Classics

Mary Beard and John Henderson both lecture in Classics at the University of Cambridge. Mary Beard is a fellow of Newnham College, and an assistant editor for the *Times Literary Supplement*. John Henderson is a fellow of King's College, Cambridge.

Praise for *Classics: A Very Short Introduction*

'For those who think Classics is just the dry as dust learning of dead languages this arresting book will come as a rude shock.... This is no potted history of Greece and Rome, but a brilliant demonstration that the continual re-excavation of our classical past is vital if the modern world is to rise to the challenge inscribed on the temple of Apollo at Delphi to "Know yourself".'

Robin Osborne
Author of *Demos: The Discovery of Classical Attica*

'Here is the great old much-maligned subject of Classics wonderfully re-invented for our times: from Arcadia to the Colosseum, from Homer to Asterix, it is, as the authors rightly say, The Greatest Show on Earth. This little book should be in the hands of every student, and every tourist to the lands of the ancient world . . . a splendid piece of work.'

Peter Wiseman
Author of *Talking to Virgil*

'Statues and slavery, temples and tragedies, museum, marbles, and mythology—this provocative guide to the Classics demystifies its varied subject-matter while seducing the reader with the obvious enthusiasm and pleasure which mark its writing.'

Edith Hall
Author of *Inventing the Barbarian*

Very Short Introductions offer stimulating, accessible introductions to a wide variety of subjects, demonstrating the finest contemporary thinking about their central problems and issues.

Also available from Oxford Paperbacks:

Politics: A Very Short Introduction
Kenneth Minogue

Archaeology: A Very Short Introduction
Paul Bahn

Buddhism: A Very Short Introduction
Damien Keown

Judaism: A Very Short Introduction
Norman Solomon

Literary Theory: A Very Short Introduction
Jonathan Culler

Islam: A Very Short Introduction
Malise Ruthven

Forthcoming in Oxford Paperbacks:

Law: A Very Short Introduction
Stephen Guest

Theology: A Very Short Introduction
David Ford

Psychology: A Very Short Introduction
Gillian Butler and Freda McManus

Music: A Very Short Introduction
Nicholas Cook

Hinduism: A Very Short Introduction
Kim Knott

Classics

Mary Beard &
John Henderson

Oxford   New York
OXFORD UNIVERSITY PRESS

Oxford University Press, Walton Street, Oxford OX2 6DP

Oxford New York
Athens Auckland Bangkok Bombay
Calcutta Cape Town Dar es Salaam Delhi
Florence Hong Kong Istanbul Karachi
Kuala Lumpur Madras Madrid Melbourne
Mexico City Nairobi Paris Singapore
Taipei Tokyo Toronto

and associated companies in
Berlin Ibadan

Oxford is a trade mark of Oxford University Press

First published as an Oxford University Press
paperback 1995

British Library Cataloguing in Publication Data
Data available

Library of Congress Cataloging in Publication Data
Beard, Mary.
   A very short introduction to classics / Mary Beard and John
Henderson.
   1. Classical literature—History and criticism. 2. Civilization,
Classical. I. Henderson, John, 1949– . II. Title.
PA3009.B4 1995   880'.09—dc20   95-18886
ISBN 0–19–285313–9

10 9 8 7 6 5 4

Printed in Great Britain
by Biddles Ltd,
Guildford and King's Lynn

Contents

List of Figures

List of Plates

List of Maps

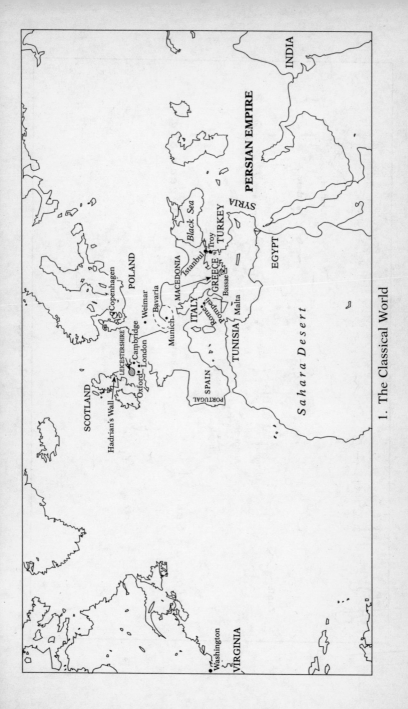

1. The Classical World

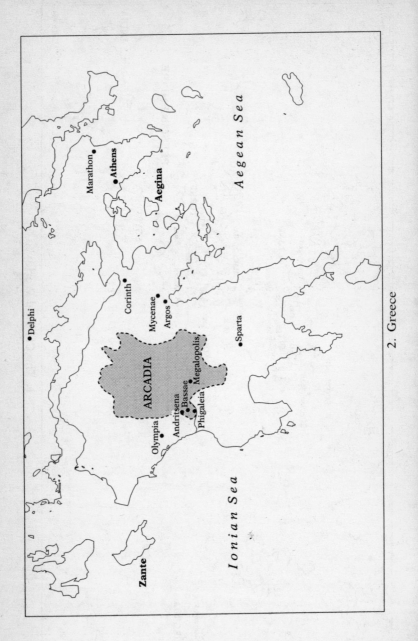

2. Greece

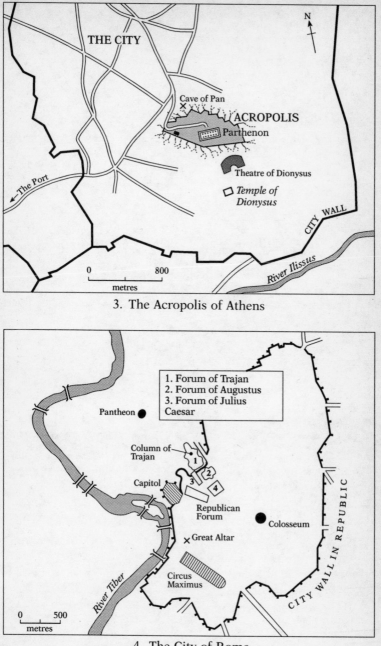

3. The Acropolis of Athens

4. The City of Rome

1 The Visit

*T*his introduction to *Classics* begins with a brief visit to a museum. We have chosen the British Museum in London, and one particular room, housing one particular monument that survives from ancient Greece. A museum is a good place to look for ancient Greece and Rome; but this visit will be the starting point for an exploration of *Classics* that extends far beyond any museum and its objects.

Our visit follows the route set out for us by the numbering on the plan provided for visitors to the museum, which the various guidebooks also follow, in sequence, through the galleries (Fig. 1). Up the grand flight of steps, through the tall columns of the classical porch, into the front hall, and past the bookshop; on through the burial urns and giant 'Ali Baba' jars that stand for heroic, pre-historic Greece (Rooms 1 and 2), and the first stiff marble figures that mark the beginning of 'classical' sculpture (Rooms 3 and 4). Then we weave our way around the cases of shiny red and black Greek vases (Room 5), until we reach the bottom of a narrow staircase, that promises to take us off the main track. (We haven't reached the prize exhibit of the Parthenon sculptures yet.) A deviation, then—and a surprise in store.

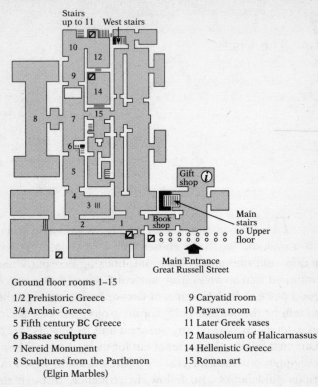

Stairs up to 11   West stairs

Ground floor rooms 1–15

1/2 Prehistoric Greece
3/4 Archaic Greece
5 Fifth century BC Greece
6 Bassae sculpture
7 Nereid Monument
8 Sculptures from the Parthenon
    (Elgin Marbles)

9 Caryatid room
10 Payava room
11 Later Greek vases
12 Mausoleum of Halicarnassus
14 Hellenistic Greece
15 Roman art

1. Plan of the British Museum: how to find the Bassae Room.

We climb the stairs to Room 6, which is on a mezzanine floor above the other galleries. Past an emotive picture of ancient ruins drawn by some 'milord' who has emphatically included the signs of his class and character—his gun and dog (see Plate 1). Our destination turns out to be a specially designed exhibition room, with carefully planned spotlights trained to set off a series of carved stone slabs, about half-a-metre high, laid end to end to form a frieze (a strip of fighting bodies, men, women, horses, half-horses . . .) that runs around the room at eye-level. (Not a centimetre to spare—this room was built to *fit*.) A couple of information panels are here to help. These sculptures, they tell us, once formed the frieze, carved towards the end of the fifth century BCE, inside the Temple of the god Apollo at a place called Bassae in Arcadia, a remote district in the south-western corner of Greece. (All the places mentioned in the book are marked on the Maps, pp. xi–xii.)

The frieze (so the panels explain) shows two of the most famous scenes of Greek myth. Half of this mass of bodies turn out to be combatants in the battle of Greeks with the half-man/half-horse Centaurs (who, in true beastly fashion, had spoiled a wedding feast by trying to steal the women); the other half are fighters in the conflict between Greeks (Greek men that is, and Herakles himself in the lead), and the wild, warrior women Amazons, strange and uncivilized. It was, the information tells us, one of the famous Twelve Labours of Herakles (in Latin, Hercules) to steal the belt of the Amazon Queen.

And the frieze is all here in the British Museum, precisely because of the English milord, and his friends, whose picture we noticed on the way up. In the early nineteenth century the remains of the temple at Bassae were rediscovered by a group of English, German, and Danish archaeologist-explorers. In a matter of months they were to make a small fortune when the sculpture was auctioned off to the British government. A few fragments have ended up in Copenhagen, a few are still in Greece; but essentially the whole thing was brought back to England.

There's a puzzle here though, as the information panel explains. This museum room may have been 'built to fit'— but to fit *what*? The twenty-three individual slabs, here neatly laid out end to end, side by side, were found widely scattered around the ruins of the temple, one by one, in complete confusion; and no one has ever been quite sure what goes with what, how to do this great stone jigsaw, or what exactly the picture is supposed to be. If you examine the drawings of the slabs of the frieze outline at the back this book (pp. 122–3), you will be following *one* solution to the problem of the original layout. What we see in the museum's Bassae Room can be no more, and no less, than someone's best guess at how it might once have looked.

At how it might once have looked? Never mind the jigsaw puzzle, the information panels have already alerted us to the fact that these sculptures, in their ancient setting, never looked much like this. In their temple they were high up, 7 metres up the wall of the inner room of the sanctuary, poorly lit, probably difficult to see (let's imagine plenty of dust and cobwebs); they were not conveniently at eye-level, spotlit for our attention. It's stating the obvious, of course, to say that we are in a museum, whose job it is to present these 'works of art' for our inspection (admiration or study), clean, tidy, and explained; stating the obvious to say that the temple at Bassae was no museum, but a religious shrine, and that these sculptures were part of a holy place, whose own visitors (as we shall see) had not come looking for labels and explanations of what they saw. (After all, *they* knew the stories of Herakles against the Amazons, Greeks against the Centaurs, from granny's knee.) There is a big gap, in other words, between the historical context and the modern display.

Museums always operate with that gap, and we museum visitors have learned to take it for granted. We are not surprised, for example, to find a prehistoric spearhead (once, maybe, lodged fatally and bloodily in the skull of some unfortunate fighter) laid out in front of us in an elegant show-case; we do not even imagine that any of those gleaming museum reconstructions of the Roman kitchen, with their wholesome ingredients and cheerful waxwork slave cooks, capture much of the (grimmer) realities of Roman, or any, cooking and domestic labour. That is how museums *are*. We are not deceived by their displays to think they 'simply' represent the past.

At the same time, that gap between the museum and the past, between us and them, prompts a series of questions. In the case of Bassae, we may be well aware that the sculptures were originally part of a religious sanctuary, not a museum. But 'religion' in what sense? How are we to think of the 'religion' practised in a Greek temple? And were 'religious' objects not also 'works of art' for the Greeks, as well as for us? This temple (as we shall discover) was in the middle of nowhere, the back of beyond, on the side of a mountain. What was the point of a temple *there*? Did no one ever come to visit it as a tourist rather than a pious pilgrim, to see the sights? Did no ancient visitor want some of the scenes, barely visible 7 metres up, *explained*? How different was a visit of theirs from our visit to the museum? How sure can we be, in other words, about the gap that separates us and them, about what we share with the fifth-century BCE visitors to this temple (pilgrims, tourists, worshippers . . . ?), and what sets us apart?

There are questions too about the histories that unfold within that gap. These sculptures are not simply objects of a story shared only by us and those who first built and used the temple. What did Bassae mean to the inhabitants of *Roman* Greece when, 300 or so years after our temple was constructed, the great superpower of ancient Rome had added Greece to the biggest empire the world had ever known? Did Roman conquest make a difference to who came to this temple, and to the expectations they had? And what of the intrepid group of explorers who braved the bandits of (then Turkish) Greece to rediscover the temple and bring its sculpture back to England? Was that an enterprise (of imperialism, of exploitation) that now embarrasses us? Were they tourists, rather like us, or not? How did Bassae fit into their vision of the classical world? Is that a vision that we can share with them, based (at least in part) on shared admiration for the literature, art, and philosophy of Greece and Rome?

Classics is a subject that exists in that gap between us and the world of the Greeks and Romans. The questions raised by *Classics* are the questions raised by our distance from 'their' world, and at the same time by our closeness to it, and by its familiarity to us. In our museums, in our literature, languages, culture, and ways of thinking. The aim of *Classics* is not only to *discover* or *uncover* the ancient world (though that is part of it, as the rediscovery of Bassae, or the excavation of the furthest outposts of the Roman empire on the Scottish borders, shows). Its aim is also to define and debate *our* relationship to that world. This book will explore that relationship, and its history, starting from a spectacle that is familiar, but, at the same time, as we shall see, can become puzzling and strange: dismembered fragments of an ancient Greek temple put on show in the heart of modern London. In Latin the word 'museum' once indicated 'a temple of the Muses'; in what respects is the modern museum the right place to preserve treasures from a classical temple? Does it only *look* the part?

The issues raised by Bassae provide a model for understanding *Classics* in its widest sense. Of course, *Classics* is about more than the physical remains, the architecture, sculpture, pottery, and painting, of ancient Greece and Rome. It is also (to select just a few things) about the poetry, drama, philosophy, science, and history written in the ancient world, and still read and debated as part of our culture. But here too, essentially similar issues are at stake, questions about how we are to read literature which has a history of more than 2,000 years, written in a society very distant and different from our own.

To read Plato's writings on philosophical topics, for example, involves facing that difference, and trying to understand a society, fourth-century BCE Greece, in which writing came not in printed books but on papyrus rolls, each one copied by the hand of a slave; and in which 'philosophy' was still thought of as an activity that went on in the open-air life of the city, and was part of a social world of drinking and dinner. Even when philosophy became a subject for study in lecture- and classroom, in its own right (as it had become to some extent by the fourth century), it remained a very different business from our own academic tradition—for all that Plato's school was the original 'Academy', named after a suburb of Athens. On the other hand, remote or not, to read Plato is also to read philosophy that belongs to us, not just to them. Plato is still the most commonly read philosopher in the world; and as we read him now, we inevitably read him as part of 'our' philosophical tradition, in the light of all those philosophers who have come since, who themselves had read Plato . . . This complex, interactive process of reading, understanding, and debate is itself the challenge of *Classics*.

The temple of Bassae is unique, unrepeatable; and the range of questions it raises is not quite like that raised by any other monument or text. This book will follow all kinds of different trails set by the temple, its sculptures, and its history: from the mythical conflicts represented on its walls (men fighting women, men fighting monsters) and the particular puzzles of its purpose, function, and use, to the slave labour that built the temple, the landscape that surrounds it, the ancient visitors who admired it, and not least, the succeeding generations who have rediscovered and reinterpreted it.

Every survival from the classical world is, of course, unique. At the same time, as this book will show, there are problems, stories, questions, significances that all those survivals hold in common; there is a place in 'our' cultural story that they (and only they) share. That, and reflection on that, amounts to *Classics*.

2 On Site

*T*he story of the rediscovery of the temple at Bassae is one of exploration, good luck, friendship, coincidence, international diplomacy, pressure salesmanship, and murder. It is also a story that reveals a lot about the different ways *Classics* might even now be defined and understood.

The story starts in Athens, in the early years of the nineteenth century. Not the sprawling modern capital, but a messy little town under Turkish rule, about 1,300 houses, not much more than a village. Certainly not a tourist centre. There was nowhere handy to stay, only a monastery, or an obliging widow if you were lucky. And there was no one to help you out, except other foreign visitors and a few long term foreign residents. In other words, you'd do well to go native and keep in step with Lord Byron, the most famous English visitor of the time (see Plate 2). Or better still you could court Louis-Sebastien Fauvel, who lived most of his life in Athens, where he held a fistful of now misleadingly grand titles, 'French Consul' for one (see Plate 5). Fauvel knew *everybody* and could wangle more or less *anything* for you, even a pass up to the great temple of the Parthenon, which then housed a mosque in the middle of the Turkish governor's fortress (long demolished to clear the temple for Greece—whether pagan or Christian, for Greece).

It was here in 1811 that the band of explorers got together: a couple of German painters-cum-architects, and two Danish archaeologists (who had all met as students in Rome), now joined by two English architects, C. R. Cockerell (see Plate 3) and John Foster, recently arrived from England via Constantinople (the modern Istanbul). Their first joint expedition was to the ruins of a temple on the island of Aegina not far from Athens. They embarked on this just as Lord Elgin's final shipments of Parthenon sculpture were being sent back to England. A nice anecdote of coincidence has them put out to sea in a small boat, passing Elgin's great ship (which also had Byron on board, returning home), serenading Byron with one of his favourite songs and being invited on board for a farewell drink or two. It was an auspicious start to a successful expedition. The temple-sculptures that they dug out of the ruins ended up, with pride of place, in Prince Ludwig I of Bavaria's new museum in his capital of Munich, where they are still on show in the Glyptothek.

Their next plan was to travel to Bassae, much further away and much more dangerous. The area round about was plagued with malaria, and the first traveller from western Europe to come across the temple (the Frenchman Joachim Bocher, in 1765) had barely lived to tell the tale. When he had tried to make a return visit shortly afterwards he was murdered by, in Cockerell's words, 'the lawless bandits of Arcadia'. Nevertheless, the group believed, from an ancient description of the temple written by a Greek traveller of the second century CE, that it had been designed by the same architect as had designed the Parthenon, *the* acknowledged masterpiece of ancient architecture. The possibility of finding another Parthenon was in their sights, and they left Athens to arrive at Bassae late in 1811.

It was Cockerell who first discovered the frieze. After a few days camped out on the hillside and poking around in the ruins, he noticed a fox coming out of its deep lair under a load of the temple debris. When he investigated he found that amongst this debris, down in the lair, was a carved marble slab, which he rightly recognized as a piece of the temple's frieze. The team carefully covered it back up again, and went away to strike a deal with the Turkish authorities, permitting them to find and remove the rest. They came back the next year, without Cockerell, who had moved on to Sicily, and one of the Danes, who had died of malaria. Raising an army of local workmen and braving attacks from bandits, most likely neighbours, if not cousins, of their workers, they dug up the frieze and other smaller pieces of sculpture, and carried them the 30-odd kilometres down to the sea, and off to the nearby island of Zante (which was then, conveniently, occupied by the British Navy). It only remained to sell them off.

One way of telling this story might be as a tale of aristocratic culture and privilege: *Classics* as the Grand Tour, the pastime of English nobility and their European equivalents (just the *names* of the Germans give it away: Baron Haller von Hallerstein, Baron Otto Magnus von Stackelberg). Upper-class boys, who had learned Latin and Greek at school, followed that up with a 'cultural' trip to Greece itself, with plenty of rowdy drinking, and scrapes over the local girls thrown in, no doubt. This was the world of an élite, rich enough to travel, and, if you think about the proceeds of the sale of the treasures, enriched by it too, and fast.

But it is more complicated than that. Think for a moment about what they were discovering Greece *for*. Some of the Bassae party had far more practical aims than our image of the Grand Tour would suggest. Cockerell himself was certainly well-heeled, but his tour had, at least in part, a professional agenda. He was an architect, looking for masterpieces of ancient building from which to learn his craft. In particular, he was curious to see how far the surviving remains of

Greek temples matched up with the recommendations of Vitruvius, an ancient Roman architect, whose architectural handbook was still in use as a professional manual. This was not just the disinterested pursuit of beauty and culture; the ancient world was offering a practical model of design, of 'how to do it', for the contemporary craftsman.

In much the same way, young artists of the period learned their skills from a study of ancient sculpture, from endless copying and re-copying of plaster casts of ancient statues, or (better still) of the originals themselves. This was not as part of a course in the *history* of art, but as a practical lesson from the best sculpture, it was believed, the world had ever produced. Today artistic training no longer relies on Greece and Rome as its main means of instruction. In fact, earlier this century plaster casts of ancient sculpture were thrown out in their hundreds by British art schools, smashed in an exaggerated effort to assert freedom from what was seen (wrongly or rightly) as the cramping constraints of such 'classical' teaching. But the role of the classical world as a practical model, whether for design, or for behaviour, still forms part of our own debates. Many of our recent architectural controversies, for example, have focused on the question of whether classical architectural forms are still the best, and most appropriate to imitate.

Think also about the motley international group that made up the expedition to Bassae: Germans, Danes, English, with the invaluable help of a Frenchman. Then remember that at the time of their discoveries Europe was in the middle of the Napoleonic Wars. This was not just a group of like-minded aristocrats; it was a group of potential enemies. *Classics*, and the rediscovery of the classical world, drew them together not only because, here outside the fray, they could share some academic and cultural interests—and never mind the war. *Classics* could represent a much more fundamental challenge to the nationalist interests of nine-teenth-century Europe.

The rediscovery of Greece was, in a way, the rediscovery of the origins of western culture as a whole. It offered a way of seeing the origin of all European civilization, that tran-scended local, nationalist squabbles. Never mind that those squabbles were always ready to rise to the surface again, when it came to auctioning off the classical treasures that had been discovered; the point was that Greece gave western culture common roots that all educated people at least could share. As we shall see in Chapter 8, it is in much the same spirit that, almost 200 years later, ancient Athens can still be seen as the ultimate ancestor of democracy world-wide, a unifying origin of a favoured political system—even if we disagree about quite what 'democracy' really means, what it has ever meant, or whose version is best. Even disputes and wars could seem, on all sides, to replay ancient battles, literally going over the same old ground; to those who received a classical education, across modern borders, events could have the feel of familiar quotations.

But the single most important fact about the expedition to Bassae is that it was an *expedition*. For centuries *Classics* has involved not just sitting in a library reading the literature that survives from the ancient world, or visiting museums to see neatly displayed sculpture. It has involved journeys of discovery, to find *Classics* and the classical world on the ground, wherever they are preserved.

So classicists have been, and still are, *explorers*. They have trekked for months over barren Turkish mountains, in search of the fortresses of the Roman conquest. They have dug out scraps of ancient papyrus, with their precious traces of ancient literature, from the sands of Egypt (once itself a province of the Roman empire). They have travelled, like Cockerell and friends, round the byways of rural Greece, drawing, measuring, and now photographing, long-forgotten classical sites. They have hired donkeys and ridden through the Syrian desert, from monastery to monastery, scouring their libraries for manuscripts in the hope of finding some lost classical text, faithfully copied by a medieval monk. To be interested in the classical world has often meant literally *to go there*, to embark on a voyage into the unknown.

That voyage, of course, is more complicated than simple *discovery* (as any explorer anywhere must always have found). It inevitably involves a tension between expectation and reality; between, in this case, an image of the glories of ancient Greece, as fountain-head of civilization, and the realities of Greece as a country to be visited. We do not know exactly what Cockerell expected when he set off on his journey from England; nor do we know his reaction on landing in Athens. But it is clear that many nineteenth-century travellers were dismayed to discover (whatever the beauties of the scenery, or the romance of the ruins) the tawdry village that stood on the site of ancient Athens, the filth and disease, and the mean dishonesty (as they saw it) of plenty of the locals. 'Tears fill the eye', wrote one early visitor, 'but not with those of delight.' As de Quincey most memorably put it, in his account of 'Modern Greece': 'What are the nuisances, special to Greece, which repel tourists from that country? They are three—robbers, fleas, and dogs.' How could such people uphold 'the glory that was Greece' in the face of its modern degradation?

There were many answers to that question. Some travellers turned their difficulties into advantage. Heroic struggles against disease, cheating, and highway robbery could be thought of as enhancing the heroism of the discovery of ancient Greece itself; swashbuckling tales of ambush, or gallant deaths in far-off climes, all added to the romance of the exploration. Others tried to see through the grim surface to the nobility of ancient Greece, still present (if somewhat hidden) in the latter-day Greeks; you could, after all, always make the Turks the real enemy (as Lord Byron did when he later returned to fight and die for Greece in the War of Independence). But others came to a very different con-clusion: that a visit to Greece was best undertaken in the imagination.

There was, in other words, a contested image of the dis-covery of the classical world. And some of the most power-ful representations of classical Greece, those which have formed the ways we still see and understand the classical past, were the creations of men who had never visited Greece itself, whose Greece was, quite plainly, 'imaginary'. John Keats, for example, whose poetry celebrated the splen-dour of Greek art and culture in early nineteenth-century England (most famously, perhaps, in his 'Ode on a Grecian Urn'), had visited Rome; but he never ventured to make the crossing to Greece. He had not read much ancient literature either, or at least not in any very scholarly way. He knew next to nothing of the ancient Greek language, but drew entirely on translations, and on what he could see in museums.

These different images did not sit easily next to one another. Keats himself was mercilessly ridiculed by many at the time for his ignorance of Greece and of Greek. One particularly vicious review of his poems (so vicious that it was widely believed at the time to have led to his death) dubbed him 'a Cockney rhymester', whose romantic vision of classical culture was built on not much more than his private fantasy. But Byron saw the point:

> John Keats, who was kill'd off by one critique;
> Just as he really promised something great,
> If not intelligible, without Greek
> Contrived to talk about the Gods of late,
> Much as they might be expected to speak.
> Poor fellow! His was an untoward fate.

All the same, Keats's vision of the beauty and sublimity of ancient Greece, fantasy or not, became the standard against which contemporary Greece and the remains of its classical past were typically judged.

The dispute is clearly seen in the exchanges over the removal of the Elgin marbles from the Parthenon to the British Museum. Some people, even at the time (this is not just a twentieth-century debate), saw this as scandalous mutilation of the monument, a sacrilegious robbery of the treasures of Greece. The most vociferous of the critics was Lord Byron; and it is another irony of the anecdote of the farewell party at sea with Cockerell and friends that the same Byron who was travelling back to England on the ship carrying some of Elgin's marbles had just written a vitriolic poem denouncing Elgin's desecration of the Parthenon. Byron painted the Scottish peer Elgin as the worst in a long line of vandals who had despoiled this shrine of the goddess Pallas Athene:

> But who, of all the plunderers of yon fane,
> On high, where Pallas linger'd, loth to flee
> The latest relic of her ancient reign;
> The last, the worst, dull spoiler, who was he?
> Blush, Caledonia! such thy son could be!

But even more striking is the fact that many people in England, committed to a particular vision of classical perfection, did not take to what they saw when the Parthenon sculptures eventually went on show. So different were these battered pieces of marble from the expectations the waiting public had had of the greatest monument of the classical world, that they were convinced that there had been a terrible mistake: the sculptures were not the original works of art at all, but replacements made much later, under the Roman empire.

The other crucial fact about the expedition to Bassae is that it was an expedition to Greece, not to Italy. True, some of the party had already visited Rome. And Cockerell was to do so when the end of the Napoleonic War made a visit feasible; for in 1811 both Rome and Naples were, in fact, formally closed to the English. Nevertheless, the choice of Greece, not Italy, as their land of exploration does represent a major change of direction in the late eighteenth and early nineteenth centuries: the goal of a classical visit abroad was no longer just Rome, but the more distant shores of Athens and beyond.

The idea of *Classics* as discovery in part explains this change. If the exploration of classical lands was seen in terms of a heroic journey to strange and remote places, then Rome had become a bit too tame. Earlier, maybe, exploration of Italy had been difficult and exotic. But by 1800 there were already plenty of hotels in Rome at least, relatively easy travel arrangements, guides and guidebooks; in short, the infrastructure of a thriving early tourist industry was in place. For those who wanted the excitement of the unknown, rather than an increasingly bourgeois 'holiday', the next step was Greece, with its undiscovered monuments, mountain hide-outs, and weird diseases.

But there was also another kind of logic in that progression from Italy to Greece, a logic that came from the ancient world itself. Rome was the world conqueror: a little town in central Italy that, by an extraordinary series of military victories over a period of 300 years, brought most of the known world under its control. Yet, at the same time, Roman culture was preoccupied with its debts to those it had conquered, above all to Greece. The Roman poet Horace saw the central paradox when he wrote in his *Epistle* to the Roman Emperor Augustus that the conquest of Greece had also been a conquest of Rome, because Roman civilization, art, and literature were all owed to Greece. *Graecia capta ferum uictorem cepit*. 'Fierce Rome', that is, 'had been captured by captive Greece.'

It is hard to know how far Rome was really parasitic on Greek culture, or how far Romans really were just savage barbarians until they were civilized by their Greek conquests. It is almost as hard to know what it would *mean* to say of Rome, or of any society, that it had no 'culture' of its own, that its civilization was simply borrowed. But it is certainly the case that the Romans themselves often put their relationship with Greece in those terms, tracing the origin of their art and architecture, as well as many of their forms of literature and poetry, directly back to Greece.

Horace, for example, presented his verse as following in the traditions of earlier Greek verse, even as a conscious imitation of Greek poetic themes and forms. To claim the status of a classic *Roman* poet, he proclaimed his indebtedness to Greek poetry written more than 500 years earlier, and long taught and studied in the Greek world as classics of Greek literature. Roman temples too (almost like museums) were filled with Greek works of art, and with Roman works that were copies of Greek works, or versions and variations on the same themes.

So, to discover Rome, whether on the ground, amongst the ruins, or by reading Latin literature in the library, has always meant to be led on to Greece as well and to discover the Greek world through the Roman. That is as true for us, or for nineteenth-century travellers, as it was for the Romans themselves. The excursion to Bassae was part of that *cultural* journey from Rome to Greece, just as much as it was part of a search for novelty, and for new territories of the unknown.

In fact, it turned out that Bassae was the site of a very particular object in the history of Roman culture and its origins. The favourite Roman style for decorating the capitals of their columns is known as 'Corinthian'. This title goes back to the ancient world itself; and the Roman architect Vitruvius explained it with a story that the style was an inheritance from Greece, invented by a man living in the Greek city of Corinth. It was the fanciest type of column capital known in Greece or Rome, with intricate scrolls and foliage, and it came to be a symbol of Roman grandeur, paraded on the façades of all their proudest buildings. Whatever the basis of Vitruvius' story, the earliest known example of the Corinthian capital was found in the temple at Bassae (proudly displayed in Plate 1). Discovered by Cockerell and his friends, it has not survived beyond a few fragments. One story goes that it was deliberately smashed out of spite by the Turkish authorities, when they discovered what a great haul of sculpture they had let the visitors take away. But our party had already drawn and recorded it, as the *Greek* ancestor of the most characteristic *Roman* architectural form.

For the sculpture itself, this part of the story ends in international rivalry and competition. The agents of Prince Ludwig had managed to secure all the statues taken from Aegina, helped by some hopeless bungling on the part of the British who were the other main bidders. It was *so* hopeless that some believed they had been tricked: the British agent had gone to Malta (where the material had been taken to safety out of the immediate war zone), apparently unaware that the auction was still going ahead on Zante. This made the British government all the more determined to win the Bassae marbles for Britain. An auction was held in 1814, on Zante again. Ludwig, content with the treasures of Aegina, was not now in the race. Fauvel put in a bid on behalf of the French, but this was easily outstripped by the British offer of £19,000.

The sculptures were loaded on a gunboat, and taken

'home' to the British Museum. There they have never ceased to provoke debate, not only about their artistic quality and history, but also about the politics of the exploration of Greece.

3 Being There

*W*e have all made a romantic visit to Bassae. We may never have been to Greece; but we *have* all opened tourist brochures and looked at posters, and in our imagination have made the trip to the temple in the mountains.

'Greece' now signifies many things, even more, no doubt, than it did 200 years ago. It is a country of sun, beaches, and seaside pleasures; it is a country where time doesn't matter, where old men sit for hours in cafés drinking ouzo and playing backgammon (or the bouzouki), and where the traditions of peasant hospitality still thrive. But a central part of our image of Greece is the particular combination of classical ruins and rugged mountain landscape that haunts almost every picture of Bassae. There may actually be many other areas of the world where we could find a similar scene; there are sites in the mountains of Turkey, for example, that look just like this. But, for us, that image of Bassae symbolizes 'Greece'. We do not need a caption on the picture to tell us where it is.

At the same time, that Greek landscape stands for *Classics*. The whole of Europe, as well as parts of Africa and western Asia, is dotted with ruins of its classical past. Everywhere that was once part of the Roman empire, from Scotland to the Sahara, still carries the physical traces of its ancient history. Some of the best-preserved Roman towns are in the deserts of Tunisia, with houses, temples, amphitheatres, and mosaics that more than rival the remains of Pompeii; and a monument such as Hadrian's Wall still makes a powerful impression, as it cuts clear across Northern England, where once it defined the Roman boundary between the civilized world and the barbarian territory beyond the pale. Yet for all that, our image of the classical world is still contained in that picture of the Greek temple in its wild mountain setting.

Every summer thousands of people do, in fact, visit Bassae (in Modern Greek, Βασσές, Vasses, or Vassai), turning the romantic voyage of their imagination into an on-site tour. Bassae is one of the high-spots of any journey through the Peloponnese. In the early years of this century, when you still had to make your way there by mule, an Oxford academic (L. R. Farnell, the author of the classic study of religion in the various Greek cities) was so overcome with the beauty of it all that he could claim that his visit had made him feel 'that most of my earthly aspirations were satisfied'. More recently, H. D. F. Kitto, pantheist and Professor of Greek at Bristol for much of the mid-twentieth century, tells how bitterly disappointed he was not to have been granted a vision from Apollo when he slept, on the night of the full moon, outside the temple at Bassae. Today Bassae is a stopping-off point for cruises around the Greek islands (putting into port for the day), or a comfortable detour for backpackers discovering 'unspoilt' Greece. Almost every modern guidebook expects you to make a visit, and explains how to do it and what you will find.

There is now a good tarmac road right up to the temple, and it's just a short drive through the mountains from the nearby village of Andritsena, with its tourist shops, hotels, and cafés. There is no bus; but, if you do not have a car, you can easily get a taxi to take you there. Accessibility is no longer a problem. This is a regular tourist outing, served by its own convenient, purpose-built highway, laid out at great expense, with the sole aim of getting visitors to the site and back again. Even so, the guidebooks emphatically celebrate the rugged remoteness of the place. They promise 'spectacular' scenery: the 'lofty cheerless' location of the temple, the 'snaking' path of the road, 'slithering along the cliffs'. A visit to Bassae, in other words, is still presented to us as an exploration into wild, unknown territory (see Plate 7).

This is just how it figures, for example, in an early 1970s novel by Simon Raven, *Come Like Shadows*, where Major Fielding Gray, who is re-writing a script for a film of Homer's *Odyssey*, turns up at 'Vassae', apparently in a state of collapse, 'sobbing his heart out about Greek hexameters and compressed prose equivalents, and, oh, Homer, Homer, and was he worthy . . .', but actually detained, drugged, and grilled by an American agent, Aloysius Sheath who works at the site for 'the American School of Greek Studies'. While Sasha and Jules are sipping lemon juice and gin elsewhere, Sheath takes Fielding 'for a walk round the temple of Apollo the Saviour at Vassae . . . "The odd thing about this temple . . . is that it was erected in the loneliest part of the country . . . The grey columns sprouted from the grey rock" . . . Grey sky and grey scrub and grey rock. Not a man, not an animal in sight anywhere. Not a house either . . . except the House of Apollo the Saviour. "Four thousand feet up, we are . . .".'

When you arrive on the site now, however, another kind of surprise awaits you. You cannot actually *see* the temple at all. It is still there, of course. And, in fact, it stands prouder now than it did in the days of Cockerell and his friends, because many of the scattered blocks have been brought together and reconstructed into standing columns. But the whole building is entirely covered by what has been described as 'an enormous circus tent', 'a vast high-tech marquee' (see Plate 8). So it has been since 1987; and so it will stay for the foreseeable future. The romantic image of classical ruins in their rugged landscape dissolves into a quite different picture, of a huge grey marquee, spread out over metal girders, and pegged into rough concrete settings in the ground.

The guidebooks do warn the attentive reader of the surprise in store. But they do little to confront the disappointment anyone will feel at visiting a famous romantic ruin that turns out to be entirely shrouded in modern, unromantic canvas. A few books come close to suggesting that you might call off your trip altogether: 'It has to be said that visitors are likely to be disappointed. If you are not put off . . .'. Most try to offer a serious account of why this tent is needed to protect the remains: to keep off the acid rain, to provide shelter for the workmen in the long programme of restoration, or (and this is the official version) to preserve the delicate foundations from erosion by water. Some even try to turn it all to the tourist's advantage, claiming that the tent itself is impressive: 'a remarkable structure in its own right, and it does add atmosphere once inside.' Visit the girders of Greece, indeed!

At this point it is probably the *differences* between any modern visit to Bassae and the early nineteenth-century explorations that seem most striking. For Cockerell and his party it was a dangerous journey, through unhospitable, unhealthy country; they literally risked their lives, in the face of brigands and fever. For us, there are taxis, hotels, and postcards to buy in the nearby village. Bassae has become a pleasant day's outing, supported and encouraged by all the resources of Greece's biggest industry: tourism.

The early travellers hoped not just for new discoveries from the classical past, but for the chance to acquire for themselves and their country whatever they could find to take away. The relics of the past were there to be possessed and owned. Modern classical tourists, on the other hand, have been taught to restrict their acquisitive ambitions to the purchase of a few postcards and souvenirs. Today you could, in fact, be arrested if you tried to take any genuinely ancient object out of Greece—even a small pot at the bottom of your suitcase, let alone twenty-three mighty slabs of sculpted marble. The guidebooks explicitly direct the tourist towards issues of conservation, and the demanding problems, as well as the expense, of keeping the Greek heritage standing up where it belongs. The loss of Bassae's romance, we are told, is all in the cause of the site's protection. So the tent serves as a vivid reminder of changed priorities in our attitudes to the classical past more generally: from a nineteenth-century culture of acquisition and ownership, to a twentieth-century culture of loving care and preservation.

But modern tourists may have rather more in common with the earlier travellers than first appears. They share a continuing sense of the excitement of exploration, felt even on the most well-trodden tourist routes. The guidebooks, as we have seen, still write up what is now the easy coach trip or taxi ride to Bassae in much the same terms that Cockerell himself described his journey. And the same books, in offering more general advice to the tourist, still tend to treat a Greek holiday as a voyage into a strange and potentially dangerous land—even if brisk warnings about 'holiday tummy' have come to replace tragic tales of death from malaria, and advice on crooked taxi-drivers and pickpockets has replaced stories of murder by those 'lawless bandits of Arcadia'.

The guidebooks also share a common culture of acquisition, ownership, and display. It may be true that the modern traveller brings home only postcards, photographs, and cheap plastic, or expensive pottery, replicas as holiday souvenirs. But it is still an essential part of the business of tourism (in Greece or anywhere) that tourists should *take something home with them*. It is a direct result of our summer holidays that twentieth-century Britain is more littered with images of *Classics* and the classical world than nineteenth-century Britain ever was: from miniature plastic Parthenons or fancy 'Greek' pots on our mantelpieces to postcard memories of classical visits stuck on our walls.

We are also quite happy to go on visiting and admiring those major works of art that earlier Grand Tourists decided to bring home from *their* Greek explorations, whatever our qualms about the propriety of these acquisitions. In fact, it is a strange irony that the twentieth-century ideology of conservation and safe-keeping can itself be used to justify holding on to these genuine classical relics, however dubiously acquired by our nineteenth-century ancestors. One of the commonest justifications offered for keeping the Parthenon marbles in the British Museum, and not returning them to Greece, is precisely that 'we' have looked after them better than they would ever have been looked after in Greece itself.

Patronizing self-congratulation can, of course, even be exported in the form of generous first-aid for Greek sites, once archaeology, collecting, and tourism have taken their toll. Back in his novel's 'Vassae', Raven satirizes his American archaeologist poser—'with the nose of a hockey-stick'—this way: '"And yet outside Athens there is not a better preserved temple in Greece. Of course", said Aloysius Sheath, "we've helped a lot with that. They're very grateful. Now then . . . You'll notice that it has six columns front and back, and fifteen on either side instead of the usual twelve. There are thirty-seven of them still standing here, but twenty-three panels of frieze have been carted away by . . . guess whom . . . the British . . ."'.

But what links us most closely of all with earlier generations of Greek explorers is the tension we inherit from them between the expectations we have of Greece and its, maybe, disappointing reality. Cockerell and his contemporaries were struck by the difference between their idealized image of the classical world and the tawdry peasant life that they actually found. The idea of glamorous and heroic exploration was one way they had of dealing with that difference. We, of course, are the inheritors not only of the ancient ideals of classical perfection, but also of that nineteenth-century romantic vision. Inevitably, the 'real' Greece will be a surprise for us too.

Whatever our commitment to archaeological conservation, we cannot help but feel let down when our trip to romantic Bassae ends at a temple that is barely visible under its grey hood. Like the early travellers, we too are obliged to find a way of dealing with that clash between our imaginary vision of Greece and what we actually see when we get there. Whatever the origin of our preconceptions, whether we are Grand Tourists or package-holiday makers, a visit to Greece always involves reconciling those preconceptions with what we actually find. We are not normally faced with the 'atmosphere' of an *indoor* temple in the clouds; but still, a visit to Greece always involves confronting different and competing visions of *Classics* and the classical world.

We modern tourists, in other words, are both like and unlike the early travellers. Our priorities have certainly shifted, the focus of our interest in the temple and its preservation is no doubt quite different, the physical conditions of our journey have changed beyond recognition. Yet we share with our predecessors not just an experience of what remains essentially the same monument (tent or no tent); we also share a set of problems about how we are to understand our visit, and how to deal with the sometimes awkward clash between the Greece that exists in our imagination and the Greece that exists on the ground. Even more important, perhaps, the experience of Greece is not something we discover for ourselves, entirely anew; it is something that, at least in part, we inherit from those earlier travellers who experienced Greece before us.

This mixture of similarity and difference offers a powerful model for understanding *Classics* as a whole. It suggests one answer to the central question that *Classics* always raises: how far does *Classics* change? How far is *Classics* today the same as it was 100, 200, 300 years ago? How far can there ever be anything new to say or think in a subject that people have written and talked about for 2,000 years or more?

The answer, as our visit to Bassae has already suggested, is that *Classics* is always the same *and* always different. When we sit down to read the epic poetry of Homer or Virgil, the philosophy of Plato, Aristotle, or Cicero, the plays of Sophocles, Aristophanes, or Plautus, we are *sharing* that activity with all those who have read those works before. It gives us something in common with the medieval monks who devotedly copied out (and so preserved for us) hundreds of classical texts, with nineteenth-century schoolboys whose days were filled with studying 'the Classics', as well as with centuries of architects and builders throughout Europe who (like Cockerell) read their Vitruvius in order to learn how to build.

More than that, *our* experience of *Classics* is inevitably influenced by *theirs*. It is not just that the choices of those medieval monks about *what* they should copy have effectively determined what classical texts are still available for us to read; for almost all the literature that survives from the ancient world owes its preservation to their energies in copying and recopying. It is also that we experience *Classics* in the light of what previous generations have said, thought, and written about the ancient world. No other subject gives quite such rich and varied company.

We are *all* already *Classicists*, however much (or little) we think we know about the Greeks and Romans. We can never come to *Classics* as complete strangers. There is no other foreign culture that is so much part of our history. This does not necessarily mean that whatever belongs within the traditions of Greece and Rome is intrinsically superior to any other civilization; nor does it mean that the classical cultures of the ancient world were themselves uninfluenced by (for example) the Semitic and African cultures that were their neighbours. In fact, part of the contemporary appeal of *Classics* lies in the ways that ancient writers confronted the extraordinarily diverse cultural traditions of their world—debated, to put it in our terms, the multi-culturalism of their own societies. Of course, snobbery and even racism have played their parts within *Classics*; but, equally, liberalism and humanism have developed and spread under its influence.

It is precisely the centrality of *Classics* to all forms of our cultural politics that binds Western civilization to its heritage. When we look, for example, at the Parthenon for the first time, we look at it already knowing that generations of architects chose precisely that style of building for the museums, town-halls, and banks of most of our major cities. When we pick up Virgil's *Aeneid* for the first time, we read it already knowing that it is a poem that has been admired, studied, and imitated for hundreds, indeed thousands, of years; that it is, in short, a *Classic*.

On the other hand, our experience of *Classics* is also new each time. *Our* reading of Virgil can never be anything like that of the medieval monk or the nineteenth-century schoolboy. In part, this follows from the different circumstances in which we read, rather like the different circumstances of travel. A visit to Bassae in a taxi is inevitably a different visit from one made on the back of an ill-tempered mule. In much the same way, reading the *Aeneid* in a handy, pocket-sized paperback is a quite different experience from reading it hand-copied, in a precious leather-bound volume; and reading it in an armchair is quite different again from reading it in class under the eye of some terrifying Victorian schoolmaster.

But the differences lie, even more strikingly, in the different questions, priorities, and assumptions that we bring to ancient texts and culture. No reader in the late twentieth century can read anything—a *Classic* or not—in the same way, or with the same understanding, as a reader of an earlier generation. Feminism, for example, has drawn attention to the complexities and importance of women within society, and recent research into the history of sexuality has also prompted radically new understanding of ancient literature and culture.

Many Victorians were no doubt entirely unsurprised by the subordination of women in both Greece and Rome, by the fact that women had no political rights in any ancient city, and by the explicit claims made by many ancient writers that a woman's role in life was to bear children, weave wool, and avoid getting talked about. At the same time Victorian scholars were busy ignoring (or even censoring) many of the passages in ancient authors that spoke, much too frankly for their tastes, about sex, between men and women, and men with boys. Modern classicists, on the other hand, do not just lament the extreme misogyny of the Greeks and Romans, or celebrate their overt eroticism, but rather explore how ancient literature sustained or questioned that misogyny, and ask what determined the ways that sex was discussed and displayed in ancient art and texts. How, for example, are we to understand what lies behind Virgil's *uarium et mutabile semper femina*, 'Women', or 'A woman, is always a kaleidoscopic and changeable thing'? These explorations are a direct result of twentieth-century debates on women's rights, theories of gender, and sexual politics; and in return *Classics* contributes vital historical depth to those twentieth-century debates.

The essential fact is that *Classics* is always *different*, as well as the *same*. This is not a simple story of *progress* in the interpretation of the ancient world. The changes in our interests no doubt involve losses as well as gains; over the last 200 years, for example, we have presumably lost a good deal of empathetic understanding of the horrors of ancient hand-to-hand fighting, and hands-on experience of the terrors of travel over uncharted seas. What matters is that those changes *make a difference*. Reading Virgil is far from an identical experience across the centuries, as we shall show in Chapter 9. No more and no less so than a visit to Bassae.

We have told our tale of modern tourism and nineteenth-century exploration to expose precisely this point, and to illustrate the complexity of the continuities and discontinuities in our experience of *Classics*. The single most important claim that we shall make in this book comes directly out of these reflections on various visits to Bassae. If *Classics* exists, as we have said, in the 'gap' between our world and the ancient world, then *Classics* is defined by *our* experience, interests, and debates as well as by *theirs*. The visit to Bassae provides a parable for understanding how varied and complex that modern contribution can be.

The importance of *our* contribution to *Classics* is brought home to us in unexpected ways. Just a few hundred metres from where we are writing this book, in the Fitzwilliam Museum in Cambridge, is a famous nineteenth-century painting of Bassae (see Plate 6). It was painted by Edward Lear, now better known for his limericks than for the paintings that provided his livelihood, who visited the site on a visit to Greece in 1848—'the most delightful six weeks tour I ever made'. Years later, when Lear was sick, house-bound, and short of money, a group of friends and well-wishers clubbed together to buy the painting and present it to the Fitzwilliam. They may have felt that it was an appropriate gift for that museum, since a plaster cast of the Bassae frieze was already on display there and Cockerell himself had been heavily involved with the design of the museum building. It would, for that matter, have been an appropriate gift for the Ashmolean Museum in Oxford, itself one of Cockerell's major works and also displaying a cast of the Bassae frieze on its main staircase.

The painting sums up the romantic image of Bassae: the desolation of the landscape, the lonely temple seen through a frame of rocks and twisted mountain trees. This is the Bassae of Cockerell, and of our guidebooks. But there is another surprise in store.

This 'Greek' landscape was actually painted in England, from the English countryside. Lear certainly made plenty of sketches when he was touring Greece; and these presumably helped to preserve the memory of the scenes and landscapes he had witnessed there. But his diaries make it quite clear that all the details of the rocks and trees in this picture were taken from life, using convenient specimens in the middle England of rural Leicestershire.

This is a vivid reminder of *our* contribution to the image of *Classics* and the classical world. Lear (and his like) quite literally constructed 'Greece' by grafting on to the recollections of his travels the local scenery of his own familiar country. But more than that, this construction helps us to understand better the tension between expectations of Greece and the reality of a visit. If we hope to find a living version of Lear's image of Bassae when we go to the site itself, how could we not be surprised or disappointed? For Lear's image was never just a faithful copy of the foreign landscape he had witnessed. Like every image of *Classics*, it was all along (in part at least) an image of his own country; part of his own culture because *Classics* was.

4   A Guide in Hand

*T*ourism lies at the very heart of *Classics*. It is not just a matter of *our* tourism to Greece, whether in the imaginary world of the travel brochures and posters, or in the real-life world of Mediterranean holidays. It is not even just a matter of the rediscovery of classical Greece by Grand Tourists like Cockerell and his friends. The Greeks and Romans were tourists too; they themselves toured the classical sites, guidebooks in hand, braving the bandits, fleeced by the locals, searching out what they had been told was most worth seeing, hungry for 'atmosphere'.

One ancient guidebook still survives: the *Guidebook to Greece* written by Pausanias in the second half of the second century CE. In ten books, Pausanias guided the assiduous traveller round what he judged to be the high-spots of Greece, on an itinerary that leads from Athens in Book I, then round Southern Greece and back up to Delphi in the North for Book X. In his eighth book he describes the region of Arcadia in the Peloponnese. One of his stops in Arcadia was the temple of Apollo at Bassae.

Taking the nearby town of Phigaleia as his starting point, he first gives, just as you would expect from any modern guidebook, the distance to Bassae; next he briefly describes the temple and its history.

ἐν δε αὐτῷ χωρίον τέ ἐστι καλούμενον Βᾶσσαι καὶ ὁ ναὸς τοῦ
Ἀπόλλωνος τοῦ Ἐπικουρίου λίθου καὶ αὐτὸς ὁ ὄροφος. ναῶν δὲ ὅσοι
Πελοποννησίοις εἰσί, μετά γε τὸν ἐν Τεγέᾳ προτιμῷτο οὗτος ἂν τοῦ
λίθου τε ἐς κάλλος καὶ τῆς ἁρμονίας ἔνεκα.

On it [Mount Cotilius] is a place called Bassae, and the temple
of Apollo the Succourer, built of stone, roof and all. Of all the
temples in the Peloponnese, next to the one at Tegea, this may
be placed first for the beauty of the stone and the symmetry of
its proportions.

He goes on to explain the particular title held by the god
Apollo at Bassae: Apollo Epikourios, the 'Succourer' or
'Helper'. This title was apparently given in recognition
of Apollo's assistance to the people of Phigaleia 'in time of
plague, just as at Athens he received the name of Averter of
Evil ['Alexikakos'] for delivering Athens also from the
plague'.

The plague he refers to was the famous one that afflicted
the Athenians at the beginning of their agonized war against
Sparta, the so-called 'Peloponnesian War', in the late fifth
century BCE. Its ghastly symptoms of fever, vomiting, and
ulceration were described in detail by Thucydides, who had
himself suffered, and recovered, from the disease. He makes
the disease a political symbol of catastrophe for democratic
Athens in his stark *History of the Peloponnesian War*: 'The
most dreadful feature of the whole affliction was not just the
loss of heart, the moment anyone realized they had caught
it—you see their minds turned to despair in a trice, they gave
themselves up for lost and put up no resistance—but as well
the way each person got infected from the fellow he was
looking after, so they died like sheep.' The same plague is
described by the Roman poet-philosopher Lucretius, who
saw in it a powerful image of cosmic disaster befalling a
human community.

Pausanias leads us to believe that the epidemic affected
this region of Southern Greece too, and that our temple was

erected at that time, presumably as a thank-offering to the god for dispelling the sickness. The identity of the architect, he suggests, confirms this link. For the temple of Bassae was designed by Iktinos, also the architect of the Parthenon in Athens, which was completed only shortly before the outbreak of the plague.

Pausanias' brief account supplies most of the potted history in our modern guidebooks. Even when they do not mention Pausanias by name, they offer the modern visitor much of his information: the plague that lay behind the temple's foundation; the link with the terrible Peloponnesian War and with the architect of the Parthenon. And, of course, it was Pausanias' account (and particularly its mention of Iktinos) that prompted Cockerell and his friends to go off in search of what they hoped would turn out to be a second Parthenon. Cockerell himself writes that 'the interesting facts recorded by Pausanias . . . were sufficient reasons to assure [himself and earlier travellers] of the importance of the investigation'.

Pausanias' own reasons for visiting Bassae are much harder to uncover. He does not explicitly say what took him up the long, dead-end mountain track, just to see this sanctuary, which was no doubt just as inaccessible in the second century CE as it was when Cockerell went there. In the course of his visit to the main city of Arcadia (Megalopolis: literally, 'Big Town') he had already seen a bronze statue of Apollo that had been removed from the temple of Bassae and put on public display some time earlier. Perhaps the sight of this had encouraged him to go and find the temple from which it had originally come. Or maybe he too was on the trail of buildings designed by the great architect of the Parthenon.

But in general terms his visit to Bassae, and his description of the temple, fit very closely with the priorities and interests he shows throughout his guidebook. Pausanias was a native of a Greek city in modern Turkey (he does not tell us exactly which). He was writing in Greek, for a Greek-speaking audience, about the geography, history, and sights of Greece. But he was also writing more than 200 years after the Roman conquest of the Greek world. It would, therefore, be just as correct to identify him as a Roman provincial, describing a tour around a long-established Roman province, for a Greek-speaking audience made up of Roman subjects or citizens. Roman conquest had meant many things for Greece, not only political subservience to Rome. By Pausanias' day the most noteworthy sights of the country would have included monuments sponsored, paid for, and erected by the ruling power: temples built with Roman money, in honour of Roman emperors; fountains, statues, markets, bathing establishments financed by Roman benefactors. Pausanias mentions a few of these, in passing, most of them recent achievements, but his focus, as at Bassae, is somewhere completely different.

Pausanias concentrates on the monuments, the history, and the culture of 'old Greece', long before the Roman conquest. His tour is in fact a historical tour of the ancient cities and sanctuaries that belonged to the distant past before Roman rule. And the stories he recounts about the monuments he visits are almost all stories that hark back to that same early period of Greek history, with its traditional customs, myths, festivals, and rituals. His account of Bassae is typical, taking the reader back to a famous plague more than 600 years before his own day, with not a single mention of any more recent event in the temple's history. Pausanias makes the *Roman* Greece of his own day almost indistinguishable, and intentionally so, from the Greece of the fifth century BCE.

The *Guidebook to Greece*, then, is more than just a practical traveller's handbook—a neutral survey of all there was to see, and how to get there. Like the writer of any guidebook, ancient or modern, Pausanias made choices about what to include, what to leave out, and *how* to describe his chosen monuments. These choices inevitably add up to more (and less) than a plain *description* of Greece. Pausanias offers readers a particular vision of Greece and Greek identity, and a particular way of experiencing Greece under Roman rule. That identity is rooted in the past before the Romans came; and the experience of Greece that he offers involves denying, or at least obscuring, Roman conquest. His guidebook, in other words, is giving a lesson in how to understand Greece. A lesson that did not depend on literally *being there*, or on actually following Pausanias on a tour round the cities and sanctuaries of Greece. Reading Pausanias could teach you a lot about *Greece*, even if you never set foot in the place. It still can.

Pausanias' account of the temple at Bassae also serves as a very important lesson for us on how precarious our knowledge of the ancient world is. Bassae is today one of the most famous and evocative of all classical sites, and this temple of Apollo one of the most commonly painted, photographed, and studied buildings in Greece. But Pausanias' few brief sentences amount to the only reference to the temple in all of the literature that survives from the ancient world. If by some chance Pausanias' *Guidebook to Greece* had been lost, if (for whatever reason) medieval scribes had not chosen this particular work to copy and preserve, we would know nothing about the temple except what the stones and sculptures themselves might suggest, once someone eventually stumbled upon them. We would have no clear idea, in other words, that it was a temple dedicated to Apollo (although the presence of Apollo and his divine sister Artemis among the figures on the frieze might, as we shall consider in Chapter 7, be a clue). We certainly would not have known anything about the title 'Epikourios', or the connection with the plague, or the involvement of the famous architect Iktinos.

Classics is full of such lucky survivals, of such near-losses. Indeed, some of the books that are now the most widely read of all ancient literature have been preserved by only the narrowest of margins. The poetry of Catullus, for example, including his famous series of love poems addressed to a woman he calls 'Lesbia', owes its survival to just one medieval manuscript copy. Likewise, Lucretius' poem *On the Nature of Things*, which tells in Latin verse of the theories of the Greek philosopher Epicurus (including an early version of an atomic theory of matter), is preserved through a single copy. And still other books, of course, have not survived at all: most of Livy's great history of Rome, for example, is lost, as are the majority of the tragedies of the great trio of Athenian tragedians, Aeschylus, Sophocles, and Euripides.

But this picture is always changing. Twenty years ago we possessed no more than a single line (quoted in another ancient writer) of one of the most renowned Roman poets, Cornelius Gallus, who was a younger contemporary of Catullus and friend of Virgil, as well as later having charge of Egypt under the emperor Augustus. But in the 1970s, in excavations in a rubbish dump of a Roman military fort in Southern Egypt, a small scrap of papyrus was discovered on which we can read eight lines of verse that are unmistakably the work of Gallus. It was perhaps thrown away by one of Gallus' own soldiers, maybe even by Gallus himself (see Plate 13).

Also from excavations in Egypt over the last hundred years, a complete play of the fourth-century BCE comic writer, Menander, and a good proportion of at least four others have come to light again. Almost all trace of his work was lost in the Middle Ages, and there are no manuscript copies of his plays. But Menander had been one of the most widely read Greek writers; and, because of the moral lessons to be learned from his plays, he was part of the daily diet of every schoolchild in the Greek-speaking world (which stretched from Greece itself to Egypt, the coast of modern Turkey and the shores of the Black Sea). It is precisely the remains of those ancient school texts of the playwright that have been rescued, dramatically enough, from the waste paper re-used to wrap Egyptian mummies.

Our knowledge of classical literature hangs on a very slender thread. Part of what we know (and don't know) can be put down to pure chance. It was sheer good fortune, for example, that archaeologists chose to excavate that particular rubbish dump at that particular Roman fort in Egypt and so found our only example of Gallus' verse. Likewise it may be just bad luck that some medieval monk spilled his wine over a manuscript he was supposed to be copying, and so obliterated all trace of the only surviving copy of a classic work. The vulnerability of ancient writings to accident, or to malpractice, has inspired both dark thoughts and a wealth of fiction. Thus Robert Graves's novels, *I, Claudius* and *Claudius the God*, re-create the lost autobiography of the Roman emperor Claudius. And in *The Name of the Rose*, Umberto Eco imagines a still more sinister version, where a monk's arson destroys his monastery library along with the only copy of the treatise by Aristotle *On Comedy*.

But the pattern of survivals is not only a matter of chance. It also depends crucially on the whole history of *Classics* and its changing interests and priorities, from the ancient world itself, through the Middle Ages, to the present day. It is not, in other words, mere luck that so many copies of Menander's plays have been found in Egypt. It is a direct consequence of the central place given to Menander in education in the Greek world. Nor is it just chance that we have so large a number of medieval manuscript copies of the *Satires* of the Roman poet Juvenal. In many of these poems Juvenal wrote vividly deploring the degraded morals of Roman society in his day (the early second century CE). They were copied and re-copied by medieval monks because they provided such trenchant denunciations of depravity, ideal material for the improving sermons of the Middle Ages: 'What street isn't awash with filthy puritans, eh? Are you cracking down on foul behaviour when you are the most notorious dyke in the gang of philosopher faggots? Hairy limbs, maybe, with stiff bristles up and down your arms, the promise of a stoical spirit, but on that smooth anus are lanced by a grinning surgeon your swollen piles.' The fact that *we* can still read Juvenal is directly connected to the uses of *Classics* in the medieval church.

Archaeology is the product of the same story. It is not just that one of the main aims in the excavation of classical sites in Egypt has precisely been the discovery of more, as yet unknown, ancient texts; though that objective certainly does lie behind much of the exploration of Egyptian sites. For a large part of the nineteenth century literature set the agenda for archaeology, determining which sites were looked for and excavated, and which sites became famous attractions. The cities of Troy and Mycenae, for example, were uncovered in the nineteenth century by Heinrich Schliemann exactly because he went looking for the cities mentioned in the great epic poem of Homer about the 'Trojan War', the *Iliad*, in the belief that he could find Agamemnon's Mycenae, and the Troy of Priam, Hector, Paris, and Helen. As we have seen, the exploration of Bassae was prompted by Pausanias' connection of the temple with the architect of the Parthenon. If Pausanias had not survived, Cockerell and his friends would never have been tempted to make the dangerous journey to this remote mountain ruin; and the British government would hardly have been tempted to buy the frieze and enshrine it in the British Museum. In many ways, the whole story we have told so far depends on Pausanias and *his* survival.

It is striking, then, that we now doubt most of the *information* on the temple of Bassae that Pausanias provides. Recent studies of the architecture of the temple, for example, have concluded, on grounds of style and date, that Iktinos himself may not have been involved in its design. And some have reckoned that Pausanias' connection of the title of Apollo with the great plague at Athens is no more than a guess, and very likely wrong. For a start, Thucydides explicitly states that the plague did not affect this area of Greece. Pausanias may have been desperately searching for any explanation for the god's unusual title of 'Helper'. The one he found, or was given, certainly gave Bassae a big plug by tying its foundation to the heyday of classical Athens, and its canonical historian.

This is another big change between *Classics* in the nineteenth century and *Classics* now. Cockerell and his contemporaries tended to see the ancient texts they read as almost unchallengeable sources of information about Greece and Rome. We, on the other hand, are ready to accept that in some cases we know better than ancient writers about the monuments, events, and history they described. We are ready to challenge Pausanias on his account of Bassae, Thucydides on his views of the causes of the disastrous Peloponnesian War, or Livy on the early history of the city of Rome. More than that, it is an important principle of *Classics* today that modern techniques of analysis can reveal more about the ancient world than the ancients knew themselves (just as one day, we accept, historians will reveal more about our own society than we can now know). It is one justification of the continuing study of *Classics* that we can improve on the knowledge of Greece and Rome that we have inherited.

Paradoxically, this gives more, not less, importance to our reading of ancient texts. What makes classical culture for us more engaging and challenging than any other ancient civilization is not simply to do with the continuing appeal of its drama or the beauty of its works of art. It is even more crucially to do with the fact that Greek and Roman writers discussed, debated, and defined their own culture, and that we can still read the texts in which they did this. Sometimes this discussion is part of the explicit project of their writing. So, for example, the 'Father of History', Herodotus, explained to late fifth-century Greek cities that their collective victory over the Persian king's invasion should be put down to the variety of what they each contributed, to their differences (in politics and culture) as much as their similarities, finding common cause only in refusing to surrender their autonomy to the un-Greek aliens from the East. And in the second century BCE the Greek historian Polybius, who was taken to Rome as a prisoner of war, set out to explain how and why it was that Rome came to dominate the whole of the Mediterranean world. But self-reflection of this kind runs implicitly through much of Greek and Roman writing. When, for example, Roman writers turn to describe the cultures of those they have conquered, again and again we find them engaged in the process of defining (implicitly at least) the nature of their own culture. That is to say, when Julius Caesar attempts to describe how different the Gauls are from the Romans, his account is also an implicit reflection on the character of Rome itself.

When we read ancient texts we are inevitably engaged in a *debate* with ancient writers who were themselves debating their own culture. It is certainly appropriate to *admire* some ancient literature. It is inevitable also that we should use ancient texts to recover *information* about the ancient world. However unreliable we think they may be, we cannot hope to know much about the ancient world without them. But *Classics* is much more than that. It is an engagement with a culture that was already engaged in reflecting on, debating, and studying both itself and the question of what it is to *be* a culture. Our experience of Bassae is embedded in a tradition of observing and thinking about that site that stretches far back beyond its nineteenth-century 'discovery' into the ancient world.

Part of the *debate* in Pausanias concerns the nature of Greek culture in the Roman empire, and so also the relationship of Greece and Rome. We have already discussed in Chapter 2 how Roman writers perceived their debt to Greece, how Roman culture defined itself (and has often been defined in the modern world) as parasitic on its Greek origins. It should now be clear that that relationship is rather more complicated than it appears at first sight. Roman culture, in other words, may be dependent on Greece; but at the same time much of our experience of Greece is mediated through Rome and Roman representations of Greek culture. Greece often comes to us through Roman eyes.

Roman visions of Greece take many forms. In the history of Greek sculpture, for example, a large number of the most famous works, those discussed and praised by ancient writers themselves, are preserved only through versions or copies made by Roman sculptors. No ancient writer celebrated the sculptures of the Bassae frieze, or those of the Parthenon frieze for that matter. It was free-standing figures, not the sculptural decoration of temples, that were the prized objects: the 'Discus Thrower' of the great fifth-century sculptor Myron, the 'Wounded Amazon' of his contemporary Pheidias, or the naked 'Aphrodite' made for the city of Cnidus by Praxiteles in the fourth century BCE. All these are known to us only as they were seen and reproduced by the Romans.

Pausanias offers a vision of Greece which, as we have seen, systematically obscures traces of Roman domination. What *we* should not obscure is the fact that Pausanias was at the same time an inhabitant of the Roman empire. Even in his effacement of Rome, he is offering a *Roman* image of Greece, as well as, inevitably, an image of Rome's empire.

This isolated temple on the side of a mountain in a remote corner of Greece is part of a much larger vision of how the whole world worked for him, as an imperial subject.

In *our* vision of Bassae too, respect for the individual history of this particular temple (unique and unrepeatable) is combined with a sense of its place in the wider history of Greece and Rome, and in our wider experience of ancient culture. Every small part of *Classics* is always written into a much bigger story.

5 Beneath the Surface

Pausanias' account of the temple at Bassae prompts us to ask what it is that we want to *know* about the classical world. In the eyes of many modern archaeologists, Pausanias stumbled blindly on his journeys around Greece. Not merely responsible for a good deal of misinformation on the sites that he chose to visit, he was also drastically limited in what he was prepared to see. His vision of the Greek world consists essentially of the great towns, with a few rural religious sites (such as Bassae) thrown in. What of Greece outside the urban centres? What of the countryside, where most of the ancient population would have lived? What of the rural markets, the farms that produced the food to support life in the cities, the peasants that worked them? Pausanias has almost nothing to tell about these.

Nor has he much to tell about that 'other' history of the sites he does include: the history of the people who built them, the funds that paid for them, the men and women who used and cared for them. It is, perhaps, in the nature of his project that details of this kind are left out. After all, which modern guidebooks devote much time to the quarrymen and labourers who made possible the buildings they so admiringly describe? None the less, for *us*, more than a moment's thought about this isolated temple in the hills inevitably raises questions about how it was constructed and what possible purpose it served. Who took the trouble to build it in this out-of-the-way place? *How* did they build it? What was it *for*?

Most modern explorers of the site, from Cockerell and his friends onwards, have wondered about the techniques that the ancient craftsmen employed to raise the precarious rows of columns so nice and straight, and keep the walls exactly aligned. How on earth was this done with only the limited tools and equipment available in the fifth century BCE? In Cockerell's own description of the temple, he provides elaborate drawings to explain the precise construction of its columns and roof, as well as a long final section giving an expert account of the intricate system of mathematical proportions that must have been used in planning the building.

The accounts by the German members of the same party also include details of rough traces of letters they found inscribed on some of the masonry blocks, presumably to remind the labourers where exactly in the building these blocks were to be placed (see Fig. 2). Recently archaeologists have studied these marks again, looking carefully at the exact form of the letters. The writing of ancient Greek letters was much less standardized than our own, and varies quite markedly according to geographical region. The letters on these blocks are unlike those normally used in the area around Bassae and have much more in common with the letters used by the Athenians. This is a clear indication that at least the skilled craftsmen involved in this building project came not from Arcadia itself, which was thought of as a pretty backward region even in the fifth century, but maybe from Athens (with Iktinos the architect?). A glimpse of the history of construction and of the people involved comes from such tiny details.

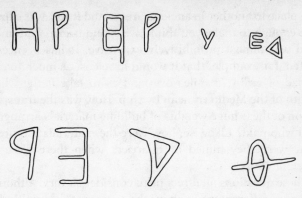

2. Greek letters left by the builders of the temple at Bassae.

The nineteenth-century explorers cannot have been unaware of other aspects of the labour required to build the temple. When they arranged the slow, mule-back journey of the twenty-three slabs of the frieze down from the mountains to the sea, they must have begun to wonder about the difficulty of bringing all that material, and much more, up to the site in the first place. Even though the cheaper local limestone that formed the main walls was quarried nearby, it would still have needed men, animals, and organization actually to bring it on site. The more expensive marble, used for the frieze and other sculpture, would have come from much further afield, with all the extra cost and labour that involved.

In fact, neither Cockerell nor any other members of his party lay much stress on the problems of supply and transportation, even though they themselves must have been acutely aware of them. Modern archaeologists and historians, by contrast, have seen such issues as absolutely central, not just for the story of Bassae, but for all classical history and culture. Transportation of almost anything from one place to another in ancient Greece and Rome was expensive enough to make you think twice, and transportation by land was almost prohibitively expensive. It has been estimated, for example, that it would have cost as much to cart a load of grain 75 miles overland as to take it the whole length of the Mediterranean by ship. How was the transportation of these huge weights of building materials arranged? And who paid? Likewise, how were the materials acquired? How were they mined or quarried, when there were no machine tools?

These questions all direct us to consider slavery. Although there are different views about the sources of the wealth that underpinned classical culture, part of the answer to every question of ancient supply and labour lies in the presence of vast numbers of slaves. Greece and Rome were notorious slave-owning societies. Perhaps the most notorious there have ever been. The privileged life of the citizen in the ancient world depended on the muscle of these human chattels, entirely without civic rights, and defined as no more than a source of labour: 'a machine with a voice' (as the first-century BCE polymath Varro put it). Numbers no doubt varied over time, and from city to city. On the best estimate, in fifth-century BCE Athens slaves formed about 40 per cent (roughly 100,000) of the total population, and in first-century BCE Italy their numbers reached almost 3 million. There can be no explanation for anything in the classical world, from mining to philosophy, from building to poetry, that does not take account of the presence of slaves.

Slavery is everywhere and obvious in Greece and Rome, and at the same time it can be difficult to see, a blind-spot both for us and for the people in the ancient world who were not slaves. Some of its traces are all too clear: the slave collars found in excavations all over the ancient world, bearing messages like a modern dog collar: 'If found, please return to . . .' (see Fig. 3); the chains and manacles dis-

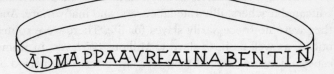

3. Roman slave-collar found around the neck of a skeleton—with the message: 'If captured return me to Apronianus, minister in the imperial palace, at the *Golden Napkin on the Aventine*, for I am a runaway slave'. (Here you can see just the address: . . . *AD MAPPA AUREA IN ABENTIN* . . .)

covered on farms in Roman Italy; the little figures depicted on Greek pots with their distinctive shaven heads, busy serving wine to their leisured citizen masters. It is obvious too in the assumptions that pervade Greek and Roman literature. Roman writers, for example, often refer in passing to the legal rule that prevented slaves from giving evidence in court unless they did so under torture. It is not just that they *could* be tortured; their evidence was only valid if they were. To the best of our knowledge, no Roman ever found anything the slightest bit odd in this.

But slavery can also be much harder to pin down than these examples might suggest. The traces of slavery are not always so easy to identify. If we think back to the masons' marks on the building blocks at Bassae, how can we actually know whose hand inscribed them? It certainly *could* have been a slave hand, the slave foreman of a slave gang brought in (from where?) for the great building operation. But it could equally well be the hand of a free craftsman, part of a skilled citizen labour force, using a slave gang for the rough work. There is simply no way of telling the status of those at work here.

Slavery was not a single, fixed category. Slaves of many different types came from many different sources: war captives, debtor peasants, home-bred children of slave mothers, educated teachers, illiterate labourers, and many more. And they were not necessarily slaves for life. There were routes out of, as well as into, slavery. Millions of slaves, in Rome especially, were granted their freedom after some period of slave service. Millions of free Roman citizens were the direct descendants of slaves. The Roman poet Horace, for example, whom we have already seen reflecting on Rome's debt to Greece, tells us from his own experience what it was like to be the son of a freed slave made good.

A small piece of bronze found at another sanctuary near Bassae captures very neatly this problem of slave visibility. Inscribed on the metal is the record of the freeing of three slaves by their master Klenis, who imposes a fine (to be paid to the god 'Apollo of Bassae' and two other local deities) on anyone who 'lays a hand on them'—that is, on anyone who fails to respect their new status. On the one hand, it is striking that even here, on the remote mountainside, we find direct evidence of the presence of slaves. Even the god Apollo in this lonely temple is implicated in the system of slavery. On the other hand, this document brings these slaves to public notice and to our attention only when they cease to be slaves. Their life *as slaves* is entirely invisible to us. We know of them only through the moment when they enter freedom.

How we should judge the system of slavery has long been one of the central questions of *Classics*. What difference does it make to our understanding of the classical world? How does it affect our admiration of (say) Athenian democracy to recognize it as a *slave-owning* democracy, and to see that it could not have been a democracy if it had not amassed a spectacular number of slaves? How far should we deplore this, or any of the other forms of cruel brutality practised in the classical world? Was it worse to be an Athenian slave or to be an Athenian woman? Is it fair to

1. Displaying the Spoils: Cockerell's image of the temple at Bassae after the excavation

2. Going Native: Byron in
Eastern dress

3. The young architect:
Charles R. Cockerell

4. Work in progress: excavation of the temple at Bassae

5. *Chez* Fauvel: the French consul at home in Athens

6. Edward Lear's *Temple of Apollo at Bassae*

7. The classic image of the temple at Bassae

8. Bassae today

9. Inside the temple: how the nineteenth century saw it

10. Herakles fights Amazon: from the Bassae frieze

11. Apollo and Artemis enter the fray: from the Bassae frieze

12. By a thread: our only manuscript of Tacitus's *Annals* XI–XVI

13. From a Roman rubbish dump: papyrus scrap with verses by
Cornelius Gallus

```
 1 ]              TRISTIA · EQVIT[.....] · LYCORI · TVA                    [
                                                                        ..[
 2 ]   FATA · MIHI · CAESAR · TVM · ERVNT · MEA · DVLCIA · QVOM · TV        [
 3 ]           MAXIMA · ROMANAE ·   RS · ERIT · HISTORIAE ·
 4 ]   POSTQVE · TVVM · REDITVM · MVLTORVM · TEMPLA · DEORVM              —[
 5 ]           FIXA · LEGAM · SPOLIEIS · DEIVITIORA · TVEIS              QVI·[
                ]                                                           [
 6    ......]..... · TA · DEM · FECERVNT  · [ .. ]MINA · MVSAE ·
 7         ... E · POSSEM · DOMINA · DEICERE · DIGNA · MEA ·
 8    ...........] ... VR · I .. M · TIBI · NON · EGO · V .. SCE ·
 9         .. ]........ L · KATO · IVDICE · TE · VEREOR
                   ]
10           ]...[                    ].
11           ]...[                    ]. · TYRIA
12                                    ].
```

14. *Ben-Hur* on stage. Poster for 'Klaw and Erlanger's stupendous production' (1901)

15. *Et in Arcadia Ego*: engraving of Reynolds's portrait of Mrs Bouverie and Mrs Crewe

judge the Greeks and Romans by our own contemporary moral standards? Or is it impossible not to?

Classics is concerned with exposing the complexities of such judgements, as well as the complexities of ancient social, economic, and political life, of which slavery was a part. It is only a first step to be able to say that (whoever actually inscribed the masons' marks) the building of the temple at Bassae must have involved a large number of slaves, in quarrying, carting, and carrying, at the very least. It is only a first step, that is, to identify this famous monument of classical culture as a product of slavery. We also need to think more broadly about all the various conditions that made the building of Bassae possible, the kind of wealth that financed it, the nature of the whole society (from slaves through peasants to aristocrats) that supported it and surrounded it.

Questions of this kind are high on the agenda of modern classical archaeology. Most archaeologists are no longer concerned with the discovery and excavation of famous classical monuments, and the treasures of ancient art that they might contain. They no longer search for the buildings of Iktinos or the sculptures of Pheidias. Their attention has shifted instead to the 'underside' of classical culture, to the life of the peasant farmers in the countryside, the general patterns of human settlement in the landscape (the small villages, the isolated farmsteads, the rural markets), the crops that were cultivated, the animals that were kept, and the food that was consumed.

This change of focus has led to a change in the kind of sites that are excavated and in the finds that are preserved and analysed. Archaeologists are now more likely to explore farms than temples. And the kind of material that used simply to be thrown away on to the dig refuse-heap is now the prize object of study. Microscopic analysis of what passed through the guts of humans or animals, and into the waste pit, can provide all sorts of information about the diet of the inhabitants and the range of crops they grew. Fragments of bone, too, can tell us not just what animals were reared, but also the age at which different types of animal were slaughtered. All this helps us to fill out a bigger picture of local agriculture; to make deductions, not just about what foodstuffs were consumed, but about what must have been imported from outside, and to measure how far trade and its profits might have been an important element in the region's economy.

The Roman city of Pompeii provides a striking instance of a change of priorities in the excavation of a single site. A hundred years ago archaeologists concentrated on uncovering the rich houses of the city, hoping particularly to discover the painting and sculpture that once decorated them. More recently they have turned their attention to the apparently open spaces of the city as well—to its gardens, market gardens, and orchards. By pouring plaster into the cavities left in the volcanic lava by the roots of the trees and plants, they have been able to identify the various species grown. This gives us, for the first time, a clear idea of the appearance of a Roman garden, and of the kinds of fruit and vegetables grown in the average Roman backyard.

Some of the questions that archaeologists now pose even lead them to giving up *digging* entirely. Broad questions about how whole tracts of land were used in the ancient world, or the pattern of settlement in a region, are answered not from excavation but from systematic survey of the modern countryside. Surveys look for any traces of ancient occupation still visible above ground, whether fragments of ancient pottery or coins lying on the surface, or standing ruins like Bassae. Field survey normally involves teams of archaeologists walking over a defined area, in lines a few metres apart from one another, and carefully plotting on a map everything they find. This method has had great success in revealing the density of ancient settlement in different sites and areas, in documenting change in land use, as well as in discovering literally hundreds of unknown rural sites. So much so that some leading archaeologists now think that, on balance, it would be best to abandon the spade altogether in favour of survey (see Fig. 4).

Field survey can answer questions about famous classical monuments as well as reveal hidden aspects of life in the classical countryside. In the case of Bassae, a survey of the surrounding area has suggested one answer to the puzzling question of what this temple, miles outside the nearest town, might actually have been *for*.

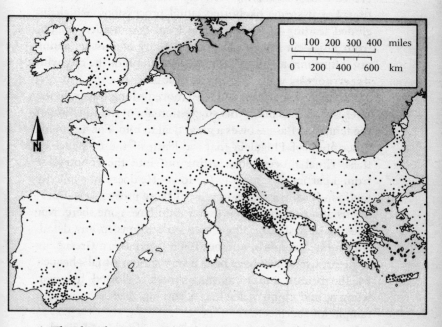

4. The distribution map has become an indispensable tool in archaeology and field survey. This example shows the pattern of urban sites across the Roman Empire.

This study has shown that the isolated sanctuary of Bassae is typical of this part of Arcadia, where there are a number of sacred sites apparently situated in the middle of nowhere, at the very edge of the territory controlled by the local town. This was a region where most of the population lived scattered through the countryside, dependent for their livelihood on rearing goats and sheep, and on hunting. The suggestion is, first, that this kind of location was absolutely appropriate for a sanctuary serving a largely rural community; and secondly, that its position on the very edge of the territory of the nearest town, Phigaleia, was crucial in rituals that united the urban political and administrative centre with the outlying territory and its scattered population. For it seems likely that ritual processions, which included leading members of the local community, set out from Phigaleia for the distant sanctuary at Bassae, acting out, affirming, and strengthening the union of the city with its territory by walking over the ground.

Although we may seem to have moved a long way from the interests of Pausanias, this suggestion about the function of the temple at Bassae owes a great deal to him. For it is in his description of Phigaleia that we learn of the existence of these ritual processions, setting out into the countryside from a particular temple in the town. He does not explicitly mention Bassae as a destination of these processions. But it seems almost certain that they would have gone there. Nor does he describe the Phigaleian processions in any detail. But in his account of another town in Southern Greece, he writes of what must have been a very similar ritual—headed by the priests and local magistrates, followed by men, women, and children leading a cow up to *their* mountain temple for sacrifice.

In other respects, too, Pausanias' *Guidebook* still lies behind many of the projects of modern archaeology and field survey. One of the themes in his account of Greece is a lament for the once-glorious cities that he visited, now barely deserving the title 'city', partly in ruins, and inhabited by just a tiny remaining population camped out in decaying buildings. This image of decline, of Greece's fall from its past prosperity, was another aspect of Pausanias' construction of an ideal Greece, back in its ancient heyday, hundreds of years before his own time. But it has also provided an important stimulus to modern archaeologists.

Recent surveys have explicitly tried to investigate Pausanias' claims of depopulation and to see how the patterns of settlement changed in Greece under Roman rule. These surveys paint a picture that partly confirms Pausanias' account, but at the same time they suggest a different way of looking at the whole problem. We now believe that it was not a simple matter of depopulation and decline. One of the effects of Roman rule, it seems, was rather to concentrate population in bigger urban centres, so producing the abandonment of some of the sites that Pausanias observed.

Classics offers a great variety of approaches, new and old, to understanding the classical past. Modern archaeology regularly draws on the newest techniques of scientific analysis, and on the newest theories of economic and social change. But it is the *combination* of these new skills with the long-known evidence of ancient writers like Pausanias that almost always makes the most impact. New methods of study do not only produce new information; they prompt us to see new significance in information recorded by writers like Pausanias, whose works may have been known, but overlooked or misunderstood, for centuries. *Classics* may involve sitting in a library reading Pausanias' *Guidebook* or searching through the remains of some ancient dung-heap. Or rather, in *Classics* these activities are seen as integral parts of the same enterprise.

6 Grand Theories

*P*ausanias' description of Bassae survived for us to read, as we have seen, through the efforts of successive generations of scribes and copyists working in an unbroken line across the millennia. Since the Renaissance, scholars have continued the work of editing and publishing classical texts. Modern books and libraries make it unlikely that any of the Greek and Roman writing that we now possess will ever be lost again. But even so the international effort continues to make available the most *authentic* texts of classical literature. Texts, that is to say, as close as possible to what was actually written 2,000 years ago.

Classical scholars travel all over Europe to track down and compare manuscripts. They scrutinize past editions and produce new ones of their own. This may involve them in the ticklish business of identifying errors made by careless copyists, that have then been reproduced in later editions; and of suggesting how those errors might be corrected to give a more accurate version of the text. Sometimes, even by the change of just a letter or two, a modern editor will present any reader who comes to consult the work with a very different idea of some fundamental aspect, or crucial detail, of the classical world.

How accurately, for example, the Romans understood the geography of the province of Britain is an important question not only for our evaluation of ancient science and techniques of mapping, but also in discussions of Roman imperialism. How much, that is, do we imagine that the Romans really *knew* about their conquered territories? The answer to this partly depends on whether you believe that the Roman historian Tacitus compared the shape of the island to a 'diamond', *scutula*, in Latin (as all the manuscripts, and most old editions, have it), or to a 'shoulder-blade', *scapula* (as an editor of the text, writing in 1967, thought would be better).

You can see why the business of producing editions of Greek and Roman authors has traditionally carried great prestige among professional scholars. It carries risks too; for the vast majority of attempts to produce a 'better' text are destined to win only temporary approval and are quickly forgotten. All the same, there is no alternative to taking the risk and *trying*, at least, to reach as accurate a view as possible of what ancient authors wrote. In fact, most obviously in works where the text is still very disputed (whether because the language itself is particularly difficult or the manuscript tradition unreliable), every single scholar who comes to study the work is inevitably involved in debates about exactly what was originally written. This is the case with some of the most famous literature to survive from the ancient world, such as the tragedies of the Athenian dramatist Aeschylus, whose texts must attract a host of suggested improvements and confessions of bafflement (see Fig. 5).

In other cases there is very little doubt that the Greek and Latin we are reading says just the same as it did when it left the writer's hand. In the poetry of Virgil and Horace, for example, carefully preserved and revered classics from the time they were written to the present day, there is not much call to improve the text. Inevitably, though, classical editors

83 Τυνδάρεω: -ρέου et -ρέα Mˢˢᶜʳ   84 Κλυταιμήϲτρα M (ut solet):
-μνήϲτρα rell. (ut solent); non amplius notatur   87 πυθοῖ F;
πευθοῖ Scaliger   θυοϲκεῖϲ Turnebus: θυοϲκινεῖϲ MVFTr, θυοϲκοεῖϲ
var. lect. in schol. vet. Tr   89 τε θυραίων Enger: τ' οὐρανίων codd.
91 δώροιϲι Tr: -οιϲ rell.   94 χρίμ- M: χρήμ- V, χρίϲμ- FTr
98 αἴνει Wieseler: αἰνεῖν MV, εἰπεῖν FTr   101 ᾶϲ ἀναφαίνειϲ
H. L. Ahrens: ἀγανὰ φαίνειϲ M, ἀγανὰ φαίνει V, ἀγανὰ φαίνουϲ' FTr
102 ἄπλειϲτον M   103 θυμοβόρον FTr (cf. Mᶻ ἥτιϲ ἐϲτὶ θυμοβόροϲ
λύπη τῆϲ φρενός)   λύπηϲ φρένα MVF: λυπόφρενα Tr; λύπηϲ φρένα
θυμοβορούϲηϲ Diggle   104 ὅϲιον κράτοϲ Ar. *Ran.* 1276 codd.
excepto R ὃϲ δῖον   105 ἐντελέων Auratus   καταπνείει Aldina:
-πνέ*ει M, -πνεύει rell. et fort. Mᵃᶜ   106 μολπᾶν Mᵃᶜ; fort. μολπᾶι
δ' ἀλκᾶν

5. The critical apparatus is an indispensable tool in editing classical texts. This example shows variant readings in surviving manuscripts, and editors' attempts to re-write a page from a tragedy by Aeschylus. All explanations are given in Latin.

cannot but be involved in *explaining* the language and content of the works they study. This explanation regularly takes the form of what is called a *commentary*, line-by-line notes on the text, which attempt to anticipate and answer the questions that readers are likely to raise. Commentaries must have many different types of reader in view, with very different levels of expertise. Many provide material for people to *learn* the Greek and Latin languages, and are careful to keep an eye out to help those who have already learned the basics to cope with difficulties in the language, as well as explaining the background in classical culture needed to understand what the ancient author wrote.

This is not a new situation. Classical scholars have always been writing for an audience that, in the main, knows no Greek or Latin. It has always been the case that Greekless and Latinless readers have needed, wanted, and demanded to be helped to find out what classical writers say, what they mean, and what that means to us. And so for centuries translations of ancient authors (often produced by the same scholars who edited the texts and wrote the commentaries) have played a major part in delivering the ancient world, and *Classics*, to the modern reader.

Some modern readers have nevertheless felt excluded from access to classical culture, precisely because they have no access to the original languages written and spoken in the ancient world. But others have been happy to use translations, and to get on with the business of becoming 'classicists' in their own language. We have already mentioned in Chapter 2 that Keats, one of the most *classical* (in every sense of the word) English poets, knew no Greek. Shakespeare too, to take another famous example, was near enough Greekless ('little Latine, and lesse Greek'). Not that he neglected classical writers. He was well-versed in the works of the Greek biographer Plutarch, who in the second century CE wrote a series of *Lives* of famous Greeks and Romans. In fact, Plutarch's *Life of Julius Caesar* was an important source for Shakespeare's *Julius Caesar*, the play in which the memorable phrase 'it was [all] Greek to me' was coined. But he read his Plutarch entirely in the English of North's translation.

Over the centuries classical texts and commentaries have changed enormously, like every other aspect of *Classics*. As *Classics* has been differently understood, and the modern world has defined its relations to the classical world differently, so commentaries written (say) at the end of the twentieth century are often concerned to direct their readers to quite different issues from those written in the 1800s. Most striking of all is the range of what has been deemed to count as *Classics*, and how boundaries between *Classics* and other disciplines have been defined and re-defined. Over the centuries questions brought to *Classics* and to classical texts have included (and still do) most of the core issues in subjects that we commonly think of as far removed from the study of Greece and Rome, but which arose directly out of work on the ancient world and its literature.

Greek philosophy, for example, and particularly the work of Plato and Aristotle, generated debates not only in what is now thought of as philosophy, but also in politics, economics, biology, and beyond. The theories of Karl Marx developed from his own training in the philosophy and history of Greece and Rome. Marx's doctoral dissertation, in fact, was a comparison of the systems of two Greek philosopher-scientists, Democritus and Epicurus, both early exponents of an atomic theory of matter. And modern anthropology, particularly through its grand theories of world culture, has a specially intimate connection with ideas produced by a series of classical scholars from the late nineteenth century on. It is this connection between *Classics* and anthropology that brings us, in an unexpected way, back to Pausanias and his *Guidebook to Greece*.

The translation we gave of Pausanias' account of Bassae in Chapter 4 was that of Sir James Frazer, founding father of modern anthropology, as well as the editor, commentator, and translator of the *Guidebook to Greece*, whose monumental six-volume edition was delivered to the world in 1898. Frazer had paid a series of visits to Greece in the early 1890s to research his *Pausanias*; and he includes in his commentary a number of lyrical passages enthusing in high Victorian style on particular landscapes, flora, and pathways, flooding the routes taken by Pausanias with his own emotionally intense style of graphic description. He even complains slightly of Pausanias' lack of interest in the scenery of the natural world: 'If he [that is, Pausanias] looks up at the mountains, it is not to mark the snowy peaks glistering in the sunlight against the blue, or the sombre pine-forests that fringe their crests, it is to tell you that Zeus or Apollo or the Sun-God is worshipped on their tops . . .' It was in the context of this project that he paid *his* visit to Bassae in 1890. He carefully inspected the site and took drawings and measurements which he later transferred to his commentary on that section of Pausanias' text.

To embark on a major edition of Pausanias was not an obvious choice for a scholar in the late nineteenth century. The *Guidebook* may have been an essential tool for early archaeologists, searching out the ancient sites of Greece. But it has never been admired for its literary quality, nor read in school or college as a central text of *Classics*. This is partly because it is a Greek work from the Roman empire, and as such has always been eclipsed both by Greek from the so-called 'classical' period of Athenian civilization (in the fifth and fourth centuries BCE) and by Latin of *its* 'classical' period, from the first century BCE to the zenith of the Roman Empire in the second century CE. It is only in much more recent times that the enormous quantity of Greek writing from the time of Pausanias on through the collapse of Rome to the rise of the Greek-speaking Byzantine empire centred on Constantinople (Istanbul) has held the attention of classical scholars, along with the welter of Latin texts, pagan and Christian, from the Later Roman Empire.

There are other factors too in the relative neglect of Pausanias outside archaeological circles. The *Guidebook* is written in unassuming note form, by a writer who is otherwise completely unknown and whose work sheds no direct light on the more central classical texts. Besides, Pausanias' careful accumulation of detailed information from site to site around the Greek mainland does not obviously engage its readers with powerful or impressive analysis on a grand scale.

But Frazer himself had particular reasons for engaging with Pausanias. What attracted him to the *Guidebook* was precisely the intricate detail in which Pausanias described not only the religious sites, public rituals, and myths of the Greek world, but also (in Frazer's words) 'the quaint customs, observances and superstitions of all sorts'. For at the time he started serious research on Pausanias, Frazer had just completed the first edition of the vast project for which he is most widely known: *The Golden Bough*. This was a work which gathered together 'quaint customs and superstitions' from all over the world and throughout history—and purported to explain them all, in one of the first and grandest of all anthropological theories that there have ever been. It was a project that grew and grew over Frazer's lifetime, from the modest two-volume edition of 1890 to the monumental third edition in twelve volumes that appeared between 1910 and 1915.

The Golden Bough, in all its different editions, opens with a *classical* problem. The puzzle that Frazer set out to explain is the strange rule that governed the priest of the goddess Diana at her sanctuary at Nemi, in the hills south of Rome. According to Roman writers, this priest, who was known by the title 'King', won his priestly office by first cutting off a branch from a particular tree in the sanctuary and then killing the previous holder of the priesthood. Each priest of Diana then lived in fear of his life, as challengers for the priesthood in turn plotted his murder. Whenever this custom started, it was still going on in the first century CE, when an ironic story tells how the Roman emperor Caligula set up a contender to go and challenge the current priest, who had held the fatal 'Kingship' too long.

Frazer's basic move was to graft this strange custom on to an episode in the middle of Virgil's *Aeneid*. He identified the branch seized by the challenger for the priesthood with the mythical 'golden bough' which allowed Virgil's hero, Aeneas, to descend safely to the world of the dead, before returning again to his mission of founding Rome. If destiny beckons Aeneas, he is told, *ipse uolens facilisque sequetur*—'The bough will come willingly and be easily plucked.' In support of this identification Frazer accumulated 'evidence' from any source, any place, any time (from Norse legends to the customs of the Australian aborigines, from Greek mythology to English corn-dollies). And as he continued, through successive editions, to add notes to his notes to his notes, he came to include references to just about the entire antiquarian and religious heritage of the whole planet, filled out by Frazer's own immensely wide reading and by contributions sent to him by legions of correspondents scattered across the globe, all contributing their own observations of corroborative material.

Frazer derived ambitious theories from all this data: theories of sacrifice, of the death and rebirth of kings (hence the importance of the title 'King' for the priest at Nemi), and of the whole intellectual development of mankind, from a primitive faith in *magic*, through *religion*, to the growth of modern *science*. In time, this central framework of his arguments entirely gave way, but the immense machine of 'knowledge' he had assembled did not collapse. As we saw was the case with Pausanias, disbelief in Frazer's *information* did not disable his project. In *The Golden Bough* he offered his readers access to universal 'knowledge' and the power that went with it, starting from the ancient world itself. That great book (which, though 'disbelieved', still sells thousands of copies in the single-volume edition each year) provides a model of the systematizing power of civilized reason. This was Frazer's great universal crusade. And it grew directly out of his labours on his classical editions, of which the *Pausanias* has proved most indispensable and, many would say, has lasted best.

It was inevitable that Frazer's project for understanding the history of human culture should have been rooted in classical scholarship and in the body of *myths* celebrated in classical texts and works of art. Across Europe these were the common property of the educated, and the material which called loudest of all for explanation. Today, when the methods of Frazer have long been discarded, the challenge remains central to *Classics*: how do we propose to think of 'Greek mythology'? Why has this repertoire of stories held such a powerful grip over so many artists and writers?

The Greek myths are still one of the most common ways that *Classics* first comes to our notice, attracting us to find out more. These stories are recounted throughout ancient literature, not just in Greek tragedy or the epic poems of Homer (the *Iliad*, and the adventures of the rascal-hero Odysseus on his long return to his home and his faithful wife Penelope), but also in the versions of these myths given by Roman writers. The Latin poet Ovid, for example, a contemporary of Virgil and Horace, wove together in his *Metamorphoses* a huge collection of all the myths of *transformation*. These were tales of 'changes of form' from the beginning of the cosmos up to his own day: the stories of Daphne changed into a laurel tree, as she fled the advances of the god Apollo of Midas' golden touch; of Julius Caesar transformed into a god at his death; and many more. Other myths he recounted in his *Fasti*, a long poem on the Roman calendar and its various religious festivals, which Frazer himself edited and translated in yet another monumental multi-volume work.

Over the last hundred years much theorizing has gone into accounting for these myths. Sigmund Freud, for example, simultaneously explored the roots of Greek mythology and the working of the human psyche when he pondered stories such as the incest of Oedipus with his mother after killing his father (so giving us the 'Oedipus complex'); or the self-infatuation of Narcissus, who fell in love with his own image as reflected in a pool of water (so giving us 'narcissism')—an unforgettable episode in Ovid's poem. The meanings found in these stories, their different versions and interpretations, proliferate, the spurious along with the inspired. This 'snow-balling' phenomenon has prompted those who study classical Greece and Rome to rethink, again and again, not just what the myths once meant, but also how that differs from (and is deepened by) their later interpretations. What difference, for example, does Freud's Oedipus make to our reading of Sophocles' play *Oedipus the King*? Must we now inevitably read Sophocles in the light of Freud?

For Frazer and his generation, however, there were other issues on the agenda of their study of Greek mythology and culture, particularly the issue of religion. In Frazer's formative years in the late nineteenth century *Classics* was studied in the framework of institutions that were more or less resolutely Christian. Universities were tiny and largely reserved for lords and ordinands; most of the dons were also clerics. Yet the glory of Greece and the grandeur of Rome were almost entirely pagan achievements. For all the dominance of the church in its teaching, *Classics* could offer a way of understanding the world that stood apart from Christianity. More than that, the authority of pagan *Classics* could be used to legitimate a whole range of radical approaches at variance with the official Christian establishment.

The religious experience of the ancient world was avidly studied, from the myths of the gods and goddesses to the ritual of public animal sacrifice and the vast range of strange local rites and lore. The Utopian worlds dreamed up by the fourth-century BCE philosopher Plato, and described particularly in his *Republic* and *Laws*, encouraged radical thinkers to institute and foster a purely secular educational philosophy. Life-values and choices forbidden by Christianity found support and political leverage in the practices and discussions of the Greeks and Romans. So, for example, Plato's discussion of the nature of love and desire, the *Symposium*, was used to justify certain forms of male homosexuality: Plato not only took for granted sexual relationships between men and boys, but (like other aristocratic contemporaries) portrayed them as the highest and noblest form of sexual desire.

All manner of eccentricities, from universal suffrage and democracy, to vegetarianism, pantheism, free love, eugenics, and genocide, found themselves precedents and authorities in *Classics*. It is a striking paradox that a late nineteenth-century guru and classicist such as Friedrich Nietzsche could rhapsodize weirdly about the cosmos being held in tension between 'Apollonian' control and 'Dionysiac' release, on the basis of the very same texts that students of *Classics* studied for the clarity of their syntax and their supposedly elevating moral earnestness.

In this world, a visit to the temple of Apollo Epikourios in the mountains of Arcadia might promise everyone their own chosen flavour of excitement, while Pausanias (with his modern 'aide' Frazer) acted as guide to the primitive, alien world before Christ. It was in the interests of many people, of course, that large parts of this pagan culture should be safely reclaimed for 'civilization'. The cost might be the re-interpreting, bowdlerizing, or, in the last resort, censoring of those aspects of classical literature that did not fit with Victorian images of a civilized culture. Thus, the notions of 'platonic love' and 'platonic relationships' derive from readings of Plato's works which nobody today could support; the adjective is the precipitate of a history of interpretation of Platonic philosophy. And the terrifying crimes and suffering displayed in Greek tragedy were determinedly taken as stern moral parables, while texts of the Athenian comic dramatist Aristophanes, prepared for use in schools and universities, regularly omitted the more explicitly sexual jokes and obscenities that are his stock in trade. Pagans could even be made Christians before their time. It was not only Dante who found Virgil an honorary place in Christendom, on the grounds that he was a 'soul *naturally* Christian'. Many nineteenth-century scholars continued to interpret one of his early poems, written more than a generation before Christ, as 'Messianic', prophesying the birth of Christ. All the same, a Frazer could always hope to find, lurking on the margins of the classical world, the 'relics' and 'vestiges' of wild savagery and strangeness.

Frazer's exposition of the dry and largely non-sensational-ized travelogue of Pausanias generated a vastly horrifying-*cum*-alluring account of the human animal close to its 'origins', before the repression of the uncivilized 'beast' by 'culture'. If Pausanias was nostalgic for the heyday of fifth-century BCE Athens, Frazer was, for his part, travelling back through time to find the natural condition of humankind, for him much the same in early Greece as in the nineteenth-century colonial backwaters still occupied by 'savages'. The story may have concluded in the triumph of modern, Chris-tian, European *reason*. But for many the thrill of using that *reason* to forage back beneath the surface of classical civili-zation was itself the attraction. Putting erotically volatile and grotesquely violent tales from Greek mythology together with notices of odd or enigmatic cultic practices peeking out from the nooks and crannies of Pausanias' Greece, could license a riot of the imagination. It still does.

Whatever the spirit of enquiry, to investigate a single sen-tence from a classical text involves contact with a host of earlier investigations. The grandest over-arching theory of the totality of existence and the most pedantic expenditure of energy on the precise analysis of mistaken words in un-trustworthy manuscripts meet up, somewhere, in the story of *Classics*.

7 The Art of Reconstruction

*P*ausanias' account of Bassae concentrates, as we have seen, on the title given there to the god Apollo: Epikourios, 'the Helper'. He already promises an explanation of this title at his first reference to the sanctuary—when he is recommending the sight of 'a four metres tall bronze statue brought [from Bassae] to adorn Megalopolis', that main town of Arcadia. When his tour reaches the spot, the *Guidebook* does indeed dwell almost exclusively on the reasons for Apollo's epithet. Although Pausanias insists in the very next paragraph that his account is the first-hand record of a visit, very little in it is drawn from observation. He tells us quickly that the temple is made of stone, roof and all, and that it ranks second of all temples in the Peloponnese for its beauty and symmetry. But there is precisely nothing about the inside of the temple, except that the statue of the god he saw in Megalopolis is no longer there. Nor does he so much as mention any of the decoration on the outside, whether sculpture or painting, despite the overall star billing he gives the building.

Modern accounts of the site have their own priorities. The salvaging of the frieze, virtually complete, and the almost total loss of the rest of the temple's sculpture have inevitably focused most attention on the frieze. But there is no consensus on what kind of attention it deserves. Pausanias' concerns, the specifically 'religious' history of the site and the 'artistic' appraisal of its adornment, still figure among *our* range of interests. But we are also concerned with what Pausanias himself may have taken for granted, or even considered beneath him to mention—in particular, the role of the temple in the lives of the local community, and what visitors saw in the mythic images carved on its stone. Just as Pausanias cannot be taken simply to represent a 'typical' ancient reaction, however, we should not pretend that any single modern view, even ours, can speak for all.

Greek and Roman temples are an emphatically conservative form of building. The basic layout is easily recognizable and found everywhere throughout the classical world from Spain to Syria: a rectangular stone platform, carrying columns spaced around a central chamber, often divided in two, front separated from back, beneath a solid roof. (For the plan of Bassae, see Fig. 6.) Particular parts of these temples regularly carried sculptural decoration. Above the columns at each end there was often a series of carved

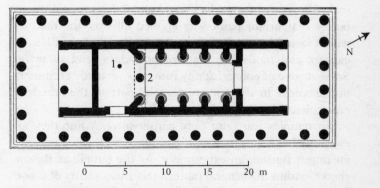

6. Ground plan of the Bassae temple, with 1: Statue of Apollo; 2: Column with Corinthian capital.

marble panels, and in the gables of the roof to front and rear a composition of sculpted figures was fitted, sometimes awkwardly, sometimes expertly, into the triangular shape formed by the slope of the eaves. Inside the main chamber, pride of place was held by the statue of the temple's god, normally facing the main doorway; but other sculpture too may have led up to this focal image, helping to declare the temple fit to house the divinity.

Much of this decoration was brightly coloured. The sculptures we now admire for their often sparkling white marble were originally painted in gaudy reds, blues, and greens. This is one of the hardest aspects of the original appearance of an ancient temple for us now to come to terms with—partly because it so violently conflicts with our image of classical perfection, or with the romantic vision of a pure white temple perched on the barren mountain shoulder. Archaeologists disagree about quite how much of any temple's sculpture was covered in paint. Analyses of surviving traces of colour are not yet conclusive. Some think that it would mostly have been added to important details, highlighted to bring them to the attention of the viewer, or just a gentle wash of colour laid over the background of a frieze to make the figures themselves stand out. Others suggest more boldly that bright paint was applied all over the marble, which would lessen the impact of the detail of the delicate carving and modelling that we nowadays tend to prize. Some degree of colour, at any rate, was certainly an important element in the ancient temple, part of the standard repertoire of its decoration.

But temples were not only conservative. While they all evidently belong to the same type, each was also a one-off, an improvisation, an experiment. As the temple at Bassae shows, within the general pattern there was plenty of scope for variation—both in the architecture and in its decoration. We will return to the frieze itself in a while. For the moment

let us concentrate on the sculptures that adorned the outside
of the building and on the overall layout of the interior. They
help us to see various different ways in which the temple
signalled its individuality.

The exterior sculptures survive, unlike the frieze, only in
small fragments. It appears that there was no sculpture in
the gables of the building; but, following the common pattern, there was a series of six carved panels (the technical
architectural term is 'metopes') above the columns at each
end. One piece of these appears to be part of a figure playing
a lyre, one of the distinctive symbols of the god Apollo (see
Fig. 7). Other fragments seem to fit together to form a male
figure draped in a cloak, similar to many representations of

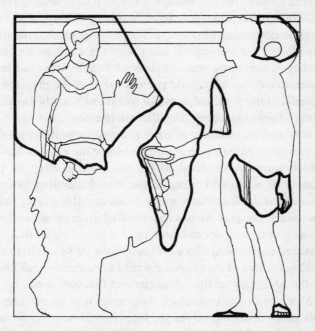

7. Reconstruction of a smashed metope. The fragment showing
Apollo 'the lyre-player' is visible in Plate 1.

the god Zeus, Apollo's father. In others there was swirling drapery, perhaps belonging to a series of dancing women. From these fragments it is impossible to be sure exactly what scenes were represented on the panels, but we have just about enough to suggest that the characters depicted made specific reference to a particular local legend.

The temple almost certainly proclaimed its identity—'the Temple of Apollo Epikourios'—by displaying the lyre-playing god (with a band of dancing nymphs or Muses) on a metope above its front door. The figure of Apollo's father Zeus, however, may well allude to one well-known story that placed this out-of-the-way region of Arcadia at the centre-stage of Greek mythology. For when Zeus was born, so the myths related, he was hidden away in a cave among these wild hills to keep him safe from his father Kronos, who was bent on destroying him—while his nurses protected the hiding-place by drowning his cries with the most *un*-musical racket. If this story was on show at Bassae, it would proclaim to anyone who could piece it together the primacy of Arcadia at the mythical origin of world order, at the installation of the rule of Zeus over the whole cosmos.

It is easy to visualize a noisy procession winding up the slopes from Phigaleia to assemble before the altar of Apollo which would have stood in the open air in front of the temple. It is easy to imagine the crowd standing in holy silence, while the priests made ready to offer prayers and sacrifice to the god. Anyone who looked up at the decoration above the temple doors could 'read' a proud claim that the civilized music of Apollo with his lyre traced its origin to the wild noise kicked up to preserve his father Zeus—back close to the beginning of time, and close to this very spot.

Much of this is conjecture. Pausanias tells us nothing of this kind—and we have started from just a few small broken pieces of marble (a hand playing a lyre, part of a torso, some fragments of a cloak) to reconstruct not only the sculpture that decorated the outside of the temple, but also something of its significance and reception. Part of the business of *Classics* is precisely this kind of *reconstruction*, the piecing together of scattered fragments to give an idea of what the whole once was like and what it meant. It *is* largely guesswork. It *is* almost always disputed. Other people, for example, have other ideas of what exactly these metopes depicted above the entrance to the temple at Bassae. But it is not *just* guesswork. It most of all depends on being able to see what remains, however fragmentary, in the context of all the other things we know about the ancient world.

Here our reconstruction depends partly on our knowledge of other surviving representations of the god Apollo—who was often depicted playing the lyre. A fragment of a hand playing a lyre in this temple is bound to suggest the figure of the god himself. But it also depends on a familiarity with the ancient myths and stories of the area, and on knowing that Arcadia was a particularly significant spot in the story of Apollo's father, Zeus. The process of piecing together the temple, in other words, leads us into the whole culture of the region.

This reconstruction of the outside decoration also shows one of the ways in which the temple claimed individuality, even within its very standard pattern. The sculptures above the entrance may have explicitly referred to the particular god associated with this temple and to particular local legends; the layout of the interior proclaims its individuality in a very different way.

The inside of a temple was used to house the image of the god and to store dedications and thank-offerings that accumulated over the centuries. It played little or no part in the ceremonies and rituals that centred on the altar outside, and the animal sacrifices that were carried out upon it. The chamber itself was a dark place. The nineteenth-century reconstruction we illustrate (Plate 9) does its best to introduce some light into the scene, by suggesting a skylight in the roof. But there is no evidence of any such arrangement, and no one today believes anything of the sort ever existed. So we should be imagining an altogether gloomier environment than is portrayed there.

In other respects, though, this reconstruction is accurate enough. The remarkable innovation of half-columns (rather than the usual rows of free-standing columns) had the effect of making the walls seem more distant, so dramatically increasing the visitor's sense of the inner dimensions of the shrine. Above them the frieze ran around the four sides of the chamber, casting eery shadows in the gloom. As visitors entered they faced straight ahead of them, just as in the picture, a single column—crucially different from all the others in the building. This is the famous 'Corinthian' column we referred to in Chapter 2, the earliest known example of a column with this particular type of capital anywhere in the ancient world (displayed in Plate 1). Here it forms a kind of screen, between the main body of the chamber and a small area beyond. In that area stood the statue of Apollo, probably in the far right-hand corner looking out through a doorway at the far left, which gave a view over the mountainside. It was probably the original statue of Apollo, four metres high, that Pausanias saw in Megalopolis, where it had been taken to adorn the town. In its place at Bassae, to judge from the scanty remains, they put another Apollo, with marble feet, hands, and head—but whose body was made out of a frame of wood, concealed by drapery. This was a much cheaper alternative to a statue of bronze, or one made entirely of marble. It would also be more likely to be left in peace in its holy of holies by powerful looters/collectors/worshippers from down in 'Big Town'.

The details of this interior layout are absolutely unique. Within the standard plan, the architects of the temple have introduced some startling features. In particular, no other temple sets a *column* at the centre of the scene, drawing every visitor's attention. No other temple places the main cult statue off the central axis, looking away towards a side door. No other temple has a sculpted frieze running all around its inner chamber. The whole building too is unusual in looking North, whereas almost all Greek temples face East.

Whatever the particular explanations for all these features, the most important point is the sheer variety of design introduced here, without losing the basic standard plan. In that respect the temple at Bassae is characteristic of much of classical culture. You could make a similar point too for other areas of *Classics*. Both Greek and Latin verse, for example, was always written to stringent rules of 'metre', which determine particular ranges of variation for patterns of 'long' and 'short' syllables throughout the whole length of a poem, even when it runs to thousands of lines (see Fig. 8). Part of the interest in reading this poetry now is to see precisely how classical poets *used* that framework, how the metrical rules incorporated difference, making innovation possible and originality recognizable, as well as setting standard patterns of versifying that every writer followed.

But it is time to consider the frieze again, in the light of what we have just said. Paradoxically (given the fact that it survives pretty much complete), the frieze raises acute pro-

$$\cup - \cup - \cup \; - \cup \cup - \cup -$$
$$\cup - \cup - \cup \; - \cup \cup - \cup -$$
$$\cup - \cup - \cup \; - \cup - \cup$$
$$- \cup \cup - \cup \cup - \cup - \cup$$

8. Classical verse can be presented in schematic form. This particular pattern of 'long' and 'short' syllables is known as the 'Alcaic stanza'. Named after its supposed inventor, the lyric poet Alcaeus, it was, with 'Sapphic stanzas', the metre commonly used in Horace's *Odes*.

blems of reconstruction. One effect of the recovery of the twenty-three slabs scattered amongst the ruins, their packaging up for transport, and their eventual reassembly for display in London, is that we have no clear evidence for their original placement or ordering in the temple. The puzzle is made particularly difficult because each slab is carved independently, with little or no overlap with any other. Most depict a tangled confusion of straining bodies. The result is that the exact layout of the frieze, which slab went next to which in the original design, is still a matter of intense disagreement among archaeologists. As we observed in Chapter 1, this jigsaw so far lacks any generally accepted solution.

All, however, agree that the frieze depicts two stories: a battle between Greeks, led by the hero Herakles, one of the many sons of Zeus, and the Amazons, a mythic race of women who lived, and fought, without men; and the fight between the mythic race of Centaurs, half-man, half-horse, and a Greek tribe called the Lapiths. It would seem obvious to suppose that each of these stories occupied two of the four sides of the complete frieze, one long side and one short side. But no one can fit the two stories neatly into that arrangement. One sequence must run into the other somewhere along at least one of the sides. This too adds to the problem of reconstruction.

But two particular scenes on two particular slabs stand out (see Plates 10 and 11). In one, Apollo draws his bow against a Centaur while his twin sister Artemis holds the reins of their chariot, drawn by stags. In the other, Herakles, draped in a lion-skin, swings his club at an Amazon who ducks away from the blow behind her shield. Many people have thought that this scene of Herakles well suits a central position, the other figures radiating to left and right. It also has vividly reminded scholars of the scene in the centre of a gable of the Parthenon in Athens (supposedly designed by the same architect), where the figures of the goddess Athene and her opponent Poseidon start back from each other in very much this way. This would then be the focal scene in this composition: positioned above the Corinthian capital, and designed to lead the visitor's eye up the column to this central moment. And if that is so, then presumably the team of Apollo and Artemis 'must' belong over the main doorway, waiting to catch our gaze as we turn to leave the chamber.

None of these details of reconstruction *need* trouble us. Nor indeed need the details of the scenes depicted. They carry the outlandish titles of 'Amazonomachy' and, even more of a mouthful, 'Lapithocentauromachy', for the Greeks *do*, as often, have a word for it, and the monster words befit their monstrous referents. But these visual stories are part of the absolutely standard repertoire of classical art and culture; they are to be found wherever classsical temple sculpture is found. At Bassae these stories set in stone and justify the claim of this hillside shrine to belong to the wide world of Greek culture, fit to take its place alongside the proudest marble monuments of any city anywhere. It is worth emphasizing, in fact, that these images certify this building as an edifice of public sanctity just as surely as the same kinds of 'classical' features certify their descendants: the banks, court-houses, museums, and official residences of any of the major cities of the modern world. Columns and gables full of classical-style sculpture still help to signal a building's public importance and solemnity: the British Museum, for example, means to be another Parthenon, and its temple-like façade parades it as a shrine, to *Classics*.

Nevertheless, the sheer ubiquity of such scenes as Greeks fighting Amazons and Lapiths fighting Centaurs does not weaken their significance. Quite the reverse: the more frequent, insistent, and prolific the representations of the myths, the more central their role in classical culture is likely to have been. Indeed, some of the most exciting work in

Classics in recent years has taken up the challenge of exploring the specific significance of just such images; and it is worth pausing for a moment to think about how this work might help us to understand and interpret what we see on the Bassae frieze itself. This will involve allowing Greek art to take us not only into the world of myth, but also much more widely into the religion, customary values, and ideology of the Greeks.

We have already proposed that the powerful scene of Herakles in conflict with an Amazon warrior took the central place of honour, above the Corinthian column. Herakles turns up everywhere you look in the classical world. At the great temple of Zeus at Olympia the twelve marble metopes, six at each end of the building, depict the twelve labours he was forced to undertake against ever-more outlandish monsters. And at Rome too, as we shall see in Chapter 9, Hercules played a major role in the national myth that enshrined the origins of Rome. The figure of Herakles/Hercules was everywhere *because* he represented some of the things that most concerned—troubled, puzzled, united, divided—both Greeks and Romans. He was, as we have learned to put it, good to think with.

When this Herakles fights his Amazon, we see a display of heroic male nudity, on frontal show—joined with his caveman's weapon, the club, and the lion-skin that he wears instead of armour and carries instead of a shield. He is strong and muscular here, but otherwise barely distinguishable from the men who fight alongside him against the Amazons, with their helmets, swords, and flying cloaks. The 'enemy' soldiers are recognizably female, their bodies decently covered by dresses except at moments of disaster; but they fight like trained troops, infantry and cavalry. Nakedness apart, the male army looks in many respects like the force which any Greek city kept ready to put into the field, but it is led and inspired by the super-male, who wandered the earth, slaying monsters to prove he is the son of Zeus.

The victory, which still hangs in the balance, will put gender back to rights. It will vindicate male courage and disarm the aliens of this monstrous regiment. And yet the wrong the Amazons do, or have done, is not clearly proclaimed. Some stories said that they invaded Greece. But Herakles also invaded *their* wild realm, sent as one of his labours to steal the belt from their queen's waist. How shall we understand what is at stake in the defeat of the Amazons? Why must these warrior women be defeated?

In part we may want to think of this as a display of male power and control over women: men wore belts to sheath swords, but women's belts were undone *by* men, for sex. Here we see in myth women who have usurped the male role of fighters and warriors, who have even claimed to construct a society entirely without men, on the brink of defeat by the forces of Greek male order. It is a strong assertion of the proper gender roles expected of Greek women and men. At the same time though, we might want to relate the struggle of Greeks and Amazons much more directly to the other story depicted on the frieze. There the Centaur guests at the wedding feast grabbed the bride, and the groom had to lead family and friends to the rescue. The Centaurs are clearly damned for their injustice, disrupting the wedding proprieties with bestial savagery; their adversaries, on the other hand, receive the authoritative assistance of Apollo and Artemis, children of Zeus.

It is tempting to see these two conflicts as closely equivalent—the combination of armed female on horseback repeated and reflected in the monstrously transgressive form of the half-man, half-horse Centaur. If this is so, then the 'crime' of the Amazons is much more than just the crime of departing from the proper behaviour expected of Greek women. In taking on the male role of fighter, the Amazons are to be seen as just as 'unnatural', just as monstrous a perversion of nature, as the monstrous Centaurs—whose behaviour strikes at the most basic rules of human society, the rules of marriage. The defeat of the Centaurs and Amazons amounts to the restoration of the 'natural' ordering of Greek society. The frieze proposes, in a sense, that the Amazons *are* the wrong which the Centaurs do.

The temple sets gender roles and the sanctity of the marital ordering of society together under divine protection. It offers a logic of how society should work that unites both gods and humans: the male must strive to follow Herakles, and achieve manhood, just as Herakles himself must fight to vindicate the paternity he shares with Apollo, effortlessly dominating his temple from behind the screen of columns. Visitors to Bassae could find a contract for human society impressed upon them—defining the roles of war and marriage, of men as the tamers of women and as their champions. And in the sequence of Apollos on view (from the lyre-player outside, through the colossal statue within, to the death-dealing archer that you saw when you left) divine power in the world could be seen as both salvation and violence, mediated through the arts of both war and music.

This kind of analysis insists that we should look very closely at what the sculpture shows, that there is more to see here than 'just' the standard repertoire of mythical battles. But it does not depend on making judgements about the artistic *quality* of the frieze as a *work of art*. It is not a question of stylistic or aesthetic success. All the same, as you examined the battered remains that our analysis has tacitly restored to their original form (we did not stop to point out that Herakles was missing a leg, or that his Amazon opponent had literally lost her head), you will probably have wondered how far you *admire* or *like* what you see in front of you.

tect of the Parthen
us to berate the loc
design.
 There have bee
frieze—Cockerell,
usually dwell on
violence, the dari
sheer brutality of
that we are badly
this imagery whe
in books, or sidle
room in the Muse
the cramped interi
at which the friez
viewed? What wc
pressive, than the
top of the visito
melées, the deep
through the gloo
 Classics involve
ment. It is still
'classical' and 'cla
to cars) are norm
the same time th
art or literature
best. Such judge
own contempora
was particularly
century there wa
phases of Greek
BCE—with their
recent years the
recognized, wh
their wayward
poets that follo

Let us make it clear at once that reaction to the sight of these slabs has been extremely mixed *from the very moment they were discovered*. You are not necessarily blind or barbarous if you find them nasty, brutish, and strangely proportioned. Fauvel, for example, at the time of the great auction of the sculptures, was apparently quite happy to write the frieze off as a second-rate purchase, fit for the British to waste their cash on. And even some of the British themselves were sceptical about the merits of what they had bought. Only a few years later Edward Dodwell, another traveller, who had himself visited the site of Bassae, wrote: 'The feet are long, the legs short and stumpy, and the extremities ridiculous in the design, and imperfect in the execution.' This was a judgement with which Frazer, in his commentary on Pausanias, heartily agreed—noting the 'grave blemishes' in the workmanship and the 'uncouth attitudes' of the figures. More recent critics too have felt much the same. For instance, a weighty handbook of Greek Art comments on the 'curiosity' of the style and the 'crude execution'.

Excuses have always been made for these poor slabs. The commonest line is that taken by the painter Benjamin Haydon, writing at the time of the sculpture's arrival in England: 'The Phygaleian marbles arrived. I saw them. Though full of gross disproportions they are beautifully composed and were evidently the design of a great genius, executed provincially.' The underlying idea here is that the frieze can claim its share in the glory of Greek civilization, that there is a glimmer of the same artistic brilliance that we recognize in the great works of Athenian art (the masterpieces of Pheidias on the Parthenon, for example); but that the work at Bassae has been dulled and diluted by the provincial fingers and thumbs of the benighted Arcadian bunglers that chiselled it out. Pausanias passes on to us the proud claim that Bassae was designed by Iktinos, the architect of the Parthenon, no less; his silence on the frieze allows us to berate the local peasants for failing to do justice to that design.

There have been some less equivocal admirers of the frieze—Cockerell, not surprisingly, amongst them. They usually dwell on the *energy* of the sculpture, its agitated violence, the daring and uncompromising display of the sheer brutality of the fighting. But they also rightly object that we are badly out of key with the original conception of this imagery when we pore over photographs and drawings in books, or sidle close up to the slabs at eye-level in their room in the Museum. Should we not be thinking instead of the cramped interior of Apollo's chamber and the steep angle at which the frieze, high above the visitor, would have been viewed? What would have been more appropriate, or impressive, than these high-relief figures crowding down on top of the visitor, in their garish colours and contorted melées, the deep-flickering shadows thrown by torchlight through the gloom?

Classics involves many such complicated matters of judgement. It is still the case, even today, that the adjectives 'classical' and 'classic' (when applied to anything from novels to cars) are normally terms of approval or admiration. Yet at the same time there is much debate about which works of art or literature surviving from the ancient world are the best. Such judgements are deeply affected by changes in our own contemporary culture. For example, when abstract art was particularly popular in the early years of the twentieth century there was a tendency also to value highly the earliest phases of Greek sculpture, of the seventh and sixth centuries BCE—with their massive, stylized, almost abstract forms. In recent years the wittily disrespectful genius of Ovid has been recognized, where once his talents were firmly deplored for their wayward and self-indulgent frivolity. And the epic poets that followed Virgil—who used to be dismissed for their sensational histrionics, the product of a decadent age—now appeal to many readers, both for their strident denunciation of the horrors of civil war and for their political bravery in speaking out under the repressive autocracy of the Roman empire.

As the case of Bassae shows, our judgements must also be influenced by how we reconstruct not only the objects themselves, but also their original context and reception. We will judge the frieze differently if we first consider how it would have looked in its temple-setting, then relate it to the function of the building and the customs and values of the people who built, used, and visited it. The same applies to literature as well as art. A Greek play represents a text that was read and studied in the ancient world, as it has been from the Renaissance to the present day; but these were once scripts written and performed for the first time in the special context of the theatre of Athens, and we will approach Greek drama differently once we see it in this light. Technical questions of history and reconstruction are inextricable from questions of quality and evaluation, and from our own fashions and preferences. *Classics* keeps these considerations together under constant review and debate.

8 The Greatest Show on Earth

A major book on the plays of the Athenian dramatist
Sophocles chooses to start with an evocative description of
the temple at Bassae:

High on a mountainside in a rugged and lonely part of Arcadia
stands a remote shrine to Zeus Lykaios, Wolf Zeus. Plato alludes
to a legend that human sacrifice was regularly practised there
and the celebrant who partook of the flesh turned into a wolf.
Across the valley from this grim precinct, in a spot of wild and
desolate beauty, in a place known as the 'glens', *Bassai*, a small
Greek city erected an elaborate temple to the most civilized of
its gods, Apollo Epikourios, the Helper. Approaching this temple at Bassae from the city of Phigaleia, as the ancients did, the
visitor experiences a striking visual confrontation of civilization
and savagery. Before the ancient spectator stood the ordered
geometry of columns and pediment outlined against the jagged
mountaintops which stretch far into the distance. Freestanding
and unexpected in that desolate setting, the temple seems as
arbitrary an example of pure form and human design as an Attic
amphora or the rhythms of a tragic chorus. But prominent just
beyond the temple is the mountain where a grisly and primitive
cult violated one of the first laws of human civilization as the
Greeks defined it, the taboo against cannibalism. (C. Segal,
Tragedy and Civilisation (1981), 1)

As we saw in the last chapter, this juxtaposition of savagery and refinement continued inside the temple, where the frieze showed heroic exertion in the midst of barbaric confusion and desecration, in vindication of the marriage-rites and gender roles which defined civilized Greek life; while the cult-statue in its screened inner sanctum stood shining serenely in the light of the rising sun, emanating calm succour for worshippers of Apollo and for the generality of afflicted mortals. The temple at Bassae can be seen to sum up the tensions inherent in Greek tragedy—not least in Sophocles' plays—between classical harmony and transgressive violence.

Clashes and collisions between 'nature' and 'culture' have been a strong theme in modern work on the ancient world, as we saw in Chapter 6 when we looked at Frazer's *Golden Bough* and *Pausanias*, and found him intent on the traces of wild otherness lurking beneath the veneer of civilization. This provided him with a measure of the *Progress of Civilisation* (to take the title of the sculpture lodged in the gable, as in a classical temple, above the entrance to the British Museum) as well as a cautionary lesson against any self-congratulatory complacency within the imperial mission to redeem pagan subjects from their native backwardness in the nineteenth century's scheme of the evolution of humanity. Just under the surface of the civilized triumphs of the classical world were still to be found all kinds of 'primitive' traits.

The opposition between nature and culture runs right through *Classics*, to the point where *the classical* has been defined and constituted precisely as the cool, calm, pure restraint exercised through the cosmos by Apollo, and the Greeks, in particular, seen as the originators of whatever enlightenment we can trace back from the modern Western tradition inspired by classical culture. In the aftermath of the Second World War a famous book by E. R. Dodds,

Professor of Greek at Oxford in the 1950s, *The Greeks and the Irrational*, protested that it was unreasonable to 'attribute to the ancient Greeks an immunity from "primitive" modes of thought which we do not find in any society open to our direct observation'. His book was extremely influential in showing classicists how full Greek art and literature was of images of wildness, mania, Dionysiac ecstasy. For Dodds it was not just a question of Frazer's primitive survivals, hidden under the classical veneer; classical culture itself was partly made up of such primitive elements.

Today we are perhaps more inclined to see in the Bassae frieze how precarious is the victory of Herakles over the Amazons, and how costly the Centaurs' defeat by its Lapiths. Far from protesting that 'the Greeks were not savage', we now see the intimate connections between the debate over human inhumanity within our world and similar discussions within ancient culture. Facing the worst that people can imagine doing to each other, and having done to themselves, is very much the business of the Greek tragedies written and performed in fifth-century Athens, which rate as among the most impressive and affecting of all the works to have survived from the ancient world.

The plays of Sophocles, along with Aeschylus' and Euripides', were classics already in the fourth century; they were given a strong role in educational syllabuses from that time onwards, by the far-flung communities from Macedon to Egypt, Syria, Turkey, and right to the borders of India, who taught their children to be 'Greeks'; and by the Roman élite, that taught its sons to be 'civilized' by experiencing the fruits of Greek culture. So these tragedies played a key role as explosive discussions of the norms and limits which human society and the human self must fight to maintain—or else burst asunder into unholy chaos and ruination. The power of the scripts, the quality of their ideas, and their communication of sheer horror command audiences in any theatre, as the three Greek tragedies in performance as we write, are proving to packed houses in the theatres of London's West End. Besides, any classroom can verify this, with almost any text or translation, and any cast.

Tragedies are a strange fusion of violence and wordy, stylized, debate. The stories they dramatize centre on terrible deeds and anguish. For example, in Sophocles' plays about the family of Oedipus (*Oedipus the King*, *Oedipus at Colonus*, *Antigone*), Oedipus is doomed to find that he has, in all his efforts to *escape* the curse upon him, killed his true father, married his mother, and incestuously fathered children; cursing the one who has brought plague upon his city of Thebes, this detective learns that the criminal is himself; his wife kills herself, he puts out his eyes—and he curses his brother-sons, who will later plunge their city into civil war and kill each other in combat. Even then, there are still members of the house of Oedipus to suffer and die—for, and at the hands of, each other. As each plot tightens the screw before the impending horror bursts upon the stage, songs from the chorus of dancers—songs of joy and fear, praise and lamentation—alternate with confrontations between two or three of the main character roles. These characters may declaim formal speeches to present their case; weave sinister traps with feigned humility; or engage each other in the rapid-fire of one-line exchanges. The tonal range of the poetic language is vast, and each play takes its own line, whether arch-primitive, self-mocking, even romantic on occasion.

The texts of tragedy are, however, as we remarked at the end of the last chapter, the product of a particular institutional context in the ancient city of Athens and, for all their ever-renewed energy, must be grasped as such. The tension between nature and culture within the scenario of the plots was reproduced in the scenario of the production and performance of the plays. For these tragedies were produced for the first time at festivals of the god Dionysus: elusive god of wild intoxication and all loosening of restraint. Yet here, on the appointed dates in the state-calendar, he was brought within the city's limits, part of the ordered social life of the community. The assembled citizens of Athens, in other words, sat and watched in the theatre of Dionysus on the Acropolis below the Parthenon (see Map 3). Here the god of the wild, son of a Theban mother by Almighty Zeus, presided over the illusion as Oedipus' tragic city of Thebes, the traditional enemy of Athens, was torn apart before their eyes.

More than this, the spectators were attending the theatre on very different terms from those who attend our own dramatic performances. Drama was special to Athens as an intrinsic and key institution of the *democratic* city of the later fifth century. The traditional religious ceremonies of procession, sacrifice, and priestly prayer preceded and led into the business in the theatre. There followed a series of pre-selected performances, presenting plays that had been specially devised and written for the festival, and compulsorily funded by wealthy citizens as a contribution to the city. The whole occasion took the form of a competition between these tragic performances for a prize awarded by an appointed panel of judges.

Audiences sat through the day from first light on, expected to reflect and concentrate, as part of their role as citizens of Athens. The female roles in the dramas were all played by males; so, too, the spectators were probably all men. As such, they were also the members of the democratic mass assembly whose votes decided what Athens did and stood for; and they were the jurymen of the large courts chosen by lot from the number of citizens. Other ceremonies which preceded the performances included the presentation of war-orphans who were brought up at the expense of the city, and a parade of the tribute of silver levied by Athens from her allies, or subjects, and stored in the chamber at the West end of the Parthenon. The display to the Athenians of their city's imperialist role and of its collective ideology brought political relevance to the performances. Soldiers and judges, voters and fathers, watched Athens' own chosen form of representation. In drama, the democratic city was on display.

The plays outlived the democracy that produced them. Already in the fourth century they had become classics, taken on tour by companies around the various Greek cities, in Sicily and southern Italy as well as in Greece and the Eastern Mediterranean, which had invested in de luxe stone theatres, Athens-style. By then the independence of those cities was under threat from Macedon to the north, from Philip of Macedon and then his son Alexander the Great. When Aristotle (the philosopher who tutored the young Alexander) came to write his analysis of tragedy, which has remained the single most important piece of literary criticism in Western culture into the twentieth century, he could think of the plays as a formal abstraction, setting to one side their political specifics, and categorizing them rather as a literary and theatrical *genre*. He saw a dynamic function at work between stage and audience, the production of horror and pity, admiration and empathy. This down-playing of the democratic matrix which produced Tragedy has allowed it to be admired and performed, ever since, in societies where politics have been organized very differently.

Indeed, reverence for fifth-century Athenian culture— Tragedy and the Parthenon—has consistently struggled to play down its connection with democracy, for democracy itself has become a generally embraced and positive concept only in very recent times. Before that, *Classics* mirrored the chorus of ancient voices deploring Athenian democracy as a dangerous experiment in collective responsibility which went catastrophically wrong. The seemingly miraculous defeat of the Persians by the united forces of the major Greek cities was always a stirring story, kept alive by Herodotus' historical narrative, and forever after seen as 'The glory of Greece'; but Thucydides' powerful account of the failure of Athenian democracy to win the drawn-out 'Peloponnesian War' against Sparta and the Spartan alliance stigmatized the volatile descent into mob-rule which later political theorists would pronounce endemic to any democratic system. Thucydides was himself an Athenian failure (exiled for incompetence), but his history turned on democratic Athens as a whole, denouncing it as in reality a 'tyrant city', fed on extortion and responsible for wholesale massacre of fellow Greeks and, when expedient, cynical genocide. As we noticed in Chapter 4, democracy was for Thucydides little short of a heady mass affliction and delirium which proved suicidal once its leaders jettisoned statesmanship and took to the instant fixes of demagoguery. His writing, however, embodies just that Athenian combination of irreverent intelligence and analytic grip which made possible the city's daring experiment in handing power to the people.

The tooling of the Greek language for analytic thought and theorizing made further advances in the fourth century. Philosophers deployed and developed the language in their assault on the whole range of philosophical questions, about the nature of reality, truth, society, psychology, mortality, rhetoric, ethics, and (not least) politics. Greek, and specifically Greek philosophical discourse, was quite simply the most highly developed critical apparatus available through the duration of the ancient world. It was respected as superior even by the Romans who reduced the Greek world to the rank of provinces in their World Empire, and has continued to inspire intellectual work to the present day—particularly from the nineteenth century onwards. With this discourse Greeks could debate a cosmopolitan, universalizing, view of the constants and the differences within the range of human experience.

Before Aristotle, Plato had written philosophical treatises in the form of dramatized discussions (usually now called 'dialogues') led by his unworldly teacher Socrates. Plato was writing in the fourth century BCE, several years after the death of Socrates. But the dialogues are all set back in the days before the collapse of the full democratic glory of fifth-century Athens; and all of them were predicated on the eventual 'martyrdom' of Socrates, who was put to death in 399 BCE on charges which Plato presents as just the kind of victimization to be expected from democrats' spite and irresponsibility. (The last days of Socrates, of the Peloponnesian War, and of the full Athenian democracy are dramatized, using Plato and other sources, in Mary Renault's novel *The Last of the Wine*.) The discussions probe restlessly and stratospherically into those basic and ultimate questions which Greek philosophy has made canonical for western culture to this day. They carry their readers up and away from everyday experience, envisioning perfect and ultimate truth in the 'realness' of forms that we can only glimpse, beyond the mere shadows that make up the mundane world we inhabit.

The reference to Plato in the passage we quoted at the start of this chapter is in fact to his *Republic*. This long dialogue in ten books outlines, in the guise of an attempt to define Justice, a blueprint for an ideal political order where the defects which maim societies such as Athens, summed up for Plato in the killing of Socrates, would be ironed out of existence. He aims for a steady state where no call for social change need smuggle in social disruption. Plato's fictional Socrates brings in 'Wolf Zeus' and 'cannibalism' at the point where he is characterizing, with his usual irony, what happens when the masses get themselves a champion: the instant that this hero finds it necessary or expedient to do away with a fellow citizen, he turns into a wolf, Arcadian-style: the social, *political*, cannibal now known the world over as 'The Tyrant'.

No writing by Socrates himself survives, and we cannot know how much of the argument put into his mouth in these dialogues is pure Plato, and whether any of it goes back to Socrates himself. But the tireless Socrates, as he is presented by his animator, always reaching through iconoclastic rejection of tradition and the *status quo* toward some better vision, could only be a product of the democracy of Athens, for all his rejection of democracy. And through him and the fifth-century setting of the dialogues, Plato retreats from taking a direct stance on his own fourth-century circumstances. The brew makes an explosively unstable mix of antidemocratic, closed reaction with anti-conservative, open speculation which has inspired and enraged everyone who has had a Greek or classical education. For Plato is, not least, the best *writer* of all western thinkers.

There can be no expectation of simplicity from the modern world's attitudes to ancient political systems and ideologies. But in the main, opposition between parties carrying, for example, 'Democratic' and 'Republican' banners, represents an emphatically modern investment in two particular ancient models. On the one hand, as we have seen, Athenian democracy—with, if you like, all the excesses of the Athenian *mob* (a term itself derived from the Latin *mobile uulgus*, 'volatile crowd', in late eighteenth-century English cant). On the other, the politics of the Roman Republic, which became a rallying cry in the revolutionary surge against monarchic government that linked France with New World rebellion from the British crown. For it was ancient Rome, rather than Greece, that provided statesmen and political theorists from the Renaissance to the nineteenth century with their chief conceptual weapons: Latin was for those five centuries the common currency of the West, a shared language of government and law, and a nucleus of shared reference-points distributed through the educational curriculum of *Classics*.

In outline, Roman history knew four phases. The legendary original monarchy declined into tyranny and the last king, Tarquin the Proud, was expelled by Brutus the Liberator at the end of the sixth century BCE. There followed the free Republic, which lasted for four centuries or so. This was an oligarchic regime in which members of a more or less restricted group of rich or aristocratic families were elected by the citizen body to annual magistracies. They worked under the guidance of a chamber of former magistrates who sat as the tightly hierarchized permanent advisory body, the senate. (Hence the logo '*SPQR*', for 'Senate and People of Rome'). The Republic collapsed in the first century BCE, in a series of horrendous civil wars between rival generalissimos and their armies, arguably the first World Wars in the history of the West. Julius Caesar helped to poison forever the once honourable title of *dictator* (which had been the Republic's term for a short-term crisis leader) by adopting it to cover the illegality of his *coup d'état*. But he was soon assassinated by a band of senators, led by a second Brutus. These self-proclaimed 'tyrannicides' and 'liberators' thought to save the Republic. But after further wars between Caesar's right-hand man, Mark Antony, and his adoptive heir, the latter installed the autocracy which we know as Imperial Rome, renaming himself *Caesar Augustus*, and building a dynastic future for the World State.

But Augustus did not, of course, *tell* Rome its destiny. He declared the free Republic *restored*, complete with elections and annual magistrates, and himself just the first citizen, 'first amongst equals'. When the succession after Augustus turned out to inflict, so the Romans told themselves, a sadist, a psychotic, a senile dolt, and then a crazed psychopath on their Empire, Roman history turned into a largely unmitigated procession of transgression and spectacular cruelty. The slogan of 'the grandeur of Rome' was coined in a dreadful and forgotten poem by a young Edgar Allan Poe, 'To Helen', as twin for the 'glory of Greece':

> On desperate seas long wont to roam,
> Thy hyacinth hair, thy classic face,
> Thy Naiad airs have brought me home,
> To the glory that was Greece,
> And the grandeur that was Rome.

Under this slogan we might include the lavish remains of various emperors' spending sprees, the Colosseum, the Pantheon, Trajan's Column, and the rest (see Map 4); but what has generally been *admired* in Roman culture has been the first generation of Augustus' reign. It was here, so it was believed, that revolution was stopped and peace restored under strong government, the eternally great classics of Latin Literature were written (most of Virgil and Horace's poetry, and Livy's monumental history of Rome), and a paternal monarch worked in concert with a revived aristocracy and a grateful populace.

Most European élites, up to the end of the eighteenth century at least, took the monarchic/presidential Augustan 'compromise' as the ideal political 'balance'. Yet there were other models in Rome, to emulate or abhor. People read Tacitus, the great historian of the emperors, and thrilled to his satirical indictment of the outrages perpetrated by incestuous Caligula, nymphomaniac Messalina, perverted Nero—heaven-sent materials for modern entertainment, too, whether on stage, in pulp, or on celluloid. They imagined being Cicero, the Republic's greatest orator and writer of Latin prose, as the Caesarian nightmare overwhelmed his world—and his head and writing hand were nailed by the generals' soldiers to the tribunal where he had delivered so many tirades.

Thus the US President Thomas Jefferson declared Tacitus 'the first writer in the world without exception . . . the strongest writer in the world'. And, like the French revolutionaries, the American Founding Fathers looked back, with the help of Livy, away from monarchy (however camouflaged by Augustus), to heroes of the early Roman Republic: George Washington, for example, declaredly modelled himself on Cincinnatus, famously called from the plough to be *consul* (chief magistrate), then, after saving the state, going straight back to his humble farm with never a thought of holding on to power . . . *Classics* has seen the stock of classical models rise and fall, under constant revision and recuperation, disputed both in themselves and for what they have been used to mean.

Jefferson can speak for the view which has been prevalent since his day: 'The same political parties which now agitate the U.S. have existed thro' all time. Whether the power of the people or that of the "aristoi" should prevail were questions which kept the states of Greece and Rome in eternal convulsions, as they now schismatize every people whose minds and mouths are not shut up by the gag of a despot.' But reflect here that 'power of the people' is a close translation of *either* Athenian δημοκρατία ('democracy') *or* Roman *res publica* (literally, 'public ownership'). 'Democracy' may now have emerged as the assumed ideal of every state. But the articulation of modern politics in terms of classical models has generated widely contrasting readings of the ancient world—as well as widely contrasting manipulations of our global community. These range from the 'senators' on Washington's Capitol (named after the chief hill of Rome), to the republicanism of Marxism, and the Fascism of Mussolini's Italy, where a new Augustan restoration was proclaimed for an 'imperial people'. Fascism was named from the *fasces*, a bundle of rods tied round an axe, the symbol of the power to scourge and behead disobedient citizens conferred on the magistrates of the Roman Republic. Jefferson too took this same badge of iron discipline for his and Washington's state of Virginia.

Imperial Rome has steadily lost charisma as an ideal, in favour of (some highly sanitized version of) Athenian democracy; but in the process resemblances between imperial Roman culture and our own circumstances have become more prominent. Like Athens, the Roman Republic *did* build its own theatre. But the Romans never dared a competitive format, and regularly adapted Greek scripts rather than write directly about their own culture. *Their* characteristic spectacles were the 'triumph', in which victorious generals paraded their prisoners, spoils, and troops through the city and up to the Capitol to give thanks to the god Jupiter 'Best and Greatest', and, ever more stunningly and overwhelmingly, the vast gladiatorial 'games'. Everyone knows all too well this form of spectacle, which Rome used to show itself to itself; for *'gladiators'* have become both a favourite focus of popular fascination with the ancient world and, in kitsch form (no one dies), the name of a symptomatic contemporary game-show transmitted by US television across the globe. But Roman gladiators were already kitsch too, star athletes playing out a *charade* of warfare, butchered to make a Roman holiday. Is this the fate that awaits any postimperial world? Amused to death?

The spectre of self-recognition in imperial Rome gives us, as it once gave Roman thinkers and poets, food for thought and debate. Today we may be drawn in particular to the telling contrast between, on the one hand, Athens' outspoken civic theatre and direct democracy, and on the other, the silencing of discussion and repression of the human voice in Roman parade and spectacle. Instead of votes, a yearly round of 'Bread and Circuses' massaged the public away from issues, arguments, and decisions. In the next chapter we shall consider, not the alternative world excogitated by Plato's intellectual Socrates, but an Arcadian 'elsewhere', first imagined during the early days of Augustus' rise to power. Throughout the history of *Classics*, this has offered a more promising place to think, watch, and listen, quieter than any Athenian theatre, and certainly less brutalized than the arena of the Roman metropolis.

As the saying goes, all roads lead to Rome. But Rome is also where the visit to Greece begins; it is *from* Rome that the mind longs to travel, away to that outpost of cultural order in the midst of wild nature, 'high on a mountainside in a rugged and lonely part of *Arcadia* . . .' *Classics* travels this route constantly, speculating and pondering: Which *is* the greatest show on earth?

9 Imagine That

*B*assae was at the furthest edge of Arcadia, a mountainous district in southern Greece. It bordered on the territory of cities famous throughout the ancient world: to the south was Sparta, more of a permanent armed camp than a city—'*Spartan*' in just the sense we now use the term; to the west lay Olympia, with its great sanctuary of Zeus which every four years was the centre of the most splendid festival of athletics in all of Greece—the ancestor of the modern *Olympics*; and to north and east were the busy towns of Argos and Corinth, and a little further away, Athens. Greeks thought of Arcadia, by contrast, as a wilderness where nature ruled, the haunt of Pan, the goatish god—half-beast, half-man in form. In myth Pan would sexually attack any creature within his grasp, girl, nymph, or animal. Greek artists depicted him joining in the revelry of Dionysus' ecstatic company.

Herodotus, the historian of the clash between the Greeks' David and the Persian king's Goliath, tells how a runner was sent by the Athenians to call the Spartans to help repel the invading Persian hordes. He bumped into Pan on his way through Arcadia. Even though the Spartans could not send help in time, Pan did bring assistance to the Athenians—who duly *panicked* the enemy to defeat. In return Pan received a shrine below the Acropolis at Athens, and an annual sacrifice and torch-race commemorated his help.

A later Greek version of the story added that the same runner ran from the battlefield at Marathon to bring news to the Athenians of their victory over the Persians; and that having done so he expired through exhaustion. The 'Marathon' race in our Olympic Games still commemorates this exploit—though it is not supposed to cost modern competitors their *lives*.

Pan's invention of the 'Pan-pipes' also helped to mark Arcadia as the home of music and song. Polybius, who (as we saw in Chapter 4) wrote an account in Greek, for Greeks, of the meteoric Roman conquest of the world, was himself an Arcadian, born in Megalopolis. He tells us that the land was so bleak and barren that song was all that stood between its people and a life beyond endurance.

But in Rome other notions of Arcadia were to take hold. Before writing his epic *Aeneid*, Virgil produced a collection of shorter 'pastoral' poems (the *Eclogues* or *Bucolics*). These poems evoke a world outside the historical world of cities, politics, and war; a place where herdsmen sit, as they have always sat, untroubled beneath shady trees that give shelter from the midday sun, trading songs or lamenting their ill luck in love. Meanwhile their animals rest, or take water, in the heat of the day. This idyllic setting is called 'Arcadia'.

In his Italian Arcadia, Virgil created a special 'elsewhere', where the imagination could escape mundane time and tune into the original scene of singing. It became a place where *minds* could wander, and poets and musicians have returned there ever since, re-imagining this community where song means more than status and possessions. At the same time, however, Virgil pictured his idyllic, pastoral world as a society already threatened by the catastrophic fall-out of the struggle for power in 'real' society. The city and its wars cast long shadows across the lives and songs of the herdsmen and farmers. Some face arbitrary eviction and exile; some, equally arbitrarily, are spared or even rewarded. In both cases these are the results of decisions imposed from Rome, but they far exceed the understanding of the Arcadian singers. Virgil's vision includes both the innocence of song and the threatening encroachment of massive forces bound to destroy its delicate fragility. The poet Louis MacNeice gets something of this bitter-sweet flavour when he begins his 'Eclogue for Christmas' with the line 'I meet you in an evil time', and the reply follows: 'The evil bells | Put out of our heads, I think, the thought of everything else.'

Pan and his 'Arcadian' haunts are also the theme of a famous Ode by Virgil's friend Horace; but the myth has a very different flavour in this lyric setting. The poem addresses Tyndaris, one of the succession of women who stir desire in the poet. The would-be seducer tells her that Pan (here under his Roman alias of Faunus) hops straight over from the mountains of Arcadia to keep safe his idyllic farm in the Italian hills, just outside Rome. Inviting her to the farm, he offers her thoughts of Pan's protection and his sweet piping echoing through the glens, with promises too of all the riches of the countryside, an attentive ear for her singing, and innocent glasses of wine in the shade: here she need not be wary, no passionately jealous lover will grab, tear, and rip her clothes when she has not deserved such treatment . . .

The poet's assurances insist just too much, as his words hint ever less covertly that there is a price for her accepting protection from Horace. Just as no nymph can be safe from Pan, so no human female can be safe from the 'Pan' that lurks inside every human male. Tyndaris is, in other words, being asked to accept Horace's advances, before *he* turns (as he might, or as might Pan) to terror, violence, and rape. The imagined world of Arcadia here is nothing short of a seductive fantasy, and a fantasy of seduction. This mythic world beyond the city has become a playground for male reverie, where nature threatens to unloose basic instincts. You can find a modern *female* version of this in Fiona Pitt-Kethley's uninhibited travelogue of Greece, where her quest for what she dubs 'the Pan Principle' takes her all round Pan's Arcadia. The 'romantic sight' of Bassae lures her, by day and by night, to this 'imposing temple [that has] gladdened the heart of generations of lovers'.

Classics studies the erotics embodied in ancient texts and art, whether it is parcelled up (as in this Ode) in splendid poetry, daubed in crude graffiti, or smeared on a sordid pot. And in the stories and fantasies of the ancient world we come across all kinds of varieties in the relations between the sexes, and within each sex. It is not just a matter of lusty heterosexual encounters between men and the women at their disposal. Through the centuries, unorthodox and re-pressed sexualities have been explored (and found pre-cedents) under the wing of *Classics*. Classical writing and art have offered the chance to ponder the Lesbianism associated with the women of the Greek island of Lesbos once made famous by the poetess Sappho, to shiver at the disarming beauty of a hermaphrodite's luscious bisexuality, or to shud-der at the priests of the goddess Cybele, who were obliged to hack off their own genitals the better to serve their goddess. On the other hand, chastity, celibacy, and the guarding of a daughter's virginity were also as securely lodged within the moral codes of the ancient world as in the strictest codes of Puritanism.

So *Classics* does more than flood the imaginative reper-toire of our cultural heritage. It offers an array of precedents for personal behaviour, sufficiently *unlike* those in our own experience to challenge our comprehension—though suf-ficiently *like* our own to fray our nerves and upset our cer-tainties. To read the poetry of Sappho, with its celebration of love between women, is inevitably to question the 'norms' of sexual behaviour, both ancient and modern. And even the myths of idyllic 'Arcadia' must prompt us to confront our own protocols of seduction, rape, and sexual violence.

Other Arcadias have moved in different directions. One of the glories of the Renaissance of classical civilization was the early sixteenth-century *Arcadia* by the Italian poet Jacopo Sannazaro. His fame swept across the courts of Europe as he hit on a priceless formula for captivating the goatherd and shepherdess lurking in the imagination of every duke and princess. *This* Arcadia, with its lovely nymphs and pretty young swains, rang to the lovesick strains of one *Sincero*, a youth exiled from his rightful high station in life, sighing in sweet harmonies. Operatic and hypnotic, this unhappy lover charms himself into the role of another Orpheus—the mythical musician who, after the loss of his beloved Eurydice, could yet make the trees dance and the rocks listen. Here readers of Sannazaro could find a suave rhetoric of love, a rigmarole of solace, and a land that prized poetry above all. It was a wholesome place for love to pine.

Among direct reactions to this particular vision of Arcadia were the 'Eclogues' of the English Elizabethan hero, Sir Philip Sidney. *His* Arcadia, an imaginary landscape already fractured by pain, sorrow and loss, returned to the anxieties that shadow Virgil's poems. It is a paradise that knows that it is already abandoned and spoiled, that music *fails* to heal the universe, that 'Arcadia' is as much a nightmare as an idyll—quite unable to save itself from its own madness. Sidney offers us an Arcadia of emotion and energy, that pushes the niceties of Sannazaro's charming vision aside once more.

Here, as so many times before and since, creative artists have found their visions in the writing of the classical world; and in the process, they have stressed different aspects of the 'original', offered new emphases and stamped the result with their own identity. Both Sannazaro and Sidney, in other words, draw on and imitate Virgil, and at the same time create something that is itself 'original', different, and distinctively their own. But they also offer something new to our understanding of the classical writing they take as their inspiration. For each new reading and 'imitation' invests Virgil's text with a fresh significance—significance that was there all along, no doubt, but remained unrecognizable until another artist's eye made it visible to us. Sannazaro and Sidney prompt us, that is, to see possibilities and hear echoes in Virgil's writing that would be lost without them.

This is another sense, then, in which *Classics* cannot ever be a subject safely locked away in a past, 2,000 years distant. For *Classics* continually finds richer texture in its works of art and literature—its meanings changed and renewed—from the multiplication of reactions and re-workings among its vast community of readers across the millennia.

Ironically, Virgil's early, 'Arcadian', poems would most likely not have gained classic status at Rome if their author had not lived on to write the great national epic. In his monumental *Aeneid*, Virgil addresses the Roman world of the first emperor Augustus, who reigned from 31 BCE to his death in 14 CE (when the senate promptly declared him a god). It was a world in the midst of revolutionary political change, emerging from years of civil war and just getting used to the idea that its traditional Republican system of government had irrevocably collapsed and that the future of Rome was under imperial autocracy. Effective power was to rest henceforth not with the elected magistrates of the state, or the old aristocratic families who had from time immemorial shared the control of the state between them, but with a single emperor and his dynastic succession.

Virgil speaks to this world by retelling a well-known story in which the origins of Rome are traced back to the mythology of Greece; in which the escape of a few Trojan survivors, in the aftermath of the Greek conquest of the city of Troy, ultimately leads, through a whole series of adventures and disasters on land and sea, to the founding of Rome. In Virgil's poem all the Eternal City's subsequent historical adventures, the triumphs and disasters of the centuries, are foreshadowed in the narrative of the journey from Troy to Rome, and the struggles to found the city. And, in particular, the poem shapes the figure of the founding hero, Aeneas, as an ancestor and model for the emperor Augustus.

Aeneas, then, is at the centre of a grand myth about precisely the cities, politics, and war which Virgil's Arcadian poetry tried to exclude. When Virgil brings Aeneas, now landed in Italy, to the future site of Rome, he has him arrive on the anniversary of an earlier visitor, Hercules—who had, in characteristic form, disposed of a local monster and founded a shrine (the so-called 'Greatest Altar'), where thanksgiving rites would be performed for ever after. Virgil's contemporaries knew that Augustus himself had returned to Rome on this very day, to celebrate *his* decisive victory, and the defeat of Mark Antony (together with his Egyptian queen, Cleopatra) that gave Augustus control over the whole of the Roman world. In this way, Virgil brings together Hercules, Aeneas, and Augustus, and creates the classic meditation on political power and leadership at Rome.

Nevertheless, even in the *Aeneid* Virgil underlines the idea that Arcadia still has a part to play in imagining Rome. For Aeneas is welcomed and given a guided tour of the seven hills where Rome will stand by the king, Evander, who has settled on the future site of Rome after fleeing his native country: Arcadia. At the very origins of the Eternal City, in other words, you find not just Trojan blood, but emigrants from Arcadia itself already established on the spot. This is the 'Arcadia' that is always to be found *within* Rome. For all the military might vested in Aeneas and his descendants, for all the imperatives that told the Romans always to fight the good fight, part of that imperative (so Virgil implies) is the protection of the vulnerable 'Arcadian' innocence of the loved ones of house and home, city and citizens: the 'Arcadia within'.

Virgil's myth of Rome has been the inspiration of all manner of reactions. The Fascists under Mussolini paraded his ideas in their propaganda, while Hermann Broch's great anti-Nazi novel, *The Death of Virgil*, has the poet regret ever attempting his poem; for in agonies of remorse he fears his writing has only served autocratic repression and wishes the masterpiece burned. He also senses that the world is at a crucial turning-point which his work will only obscure. Virgil, as we remarked in Chapter 6, was for Dante a 'naturally Christian' soul. And readers are bound to interpret this sense of a turning-point in world history as a premonition of Christianity, which arrived more than a generation after Virgil's death in 19 BCE. In other words, Christianity was located at the centre of a pagan world which could not appreciate the start of the revolution which would eventually overthrow the Roman Empire, and give the West the time-frame it uses to speak of events before and since: BC (= BCE) and AD (= CE). Jesus is, we should not forget, the most famous Roman provincial of all.

Modern fiction and film have found the birth of Jesus one of the main incentives for exploring the Roman world. The conflict between Roman paganism and Christianity is central in popular, mass-market images of *Classics*. The hugely successful epic film *Ben-Hur* (best known now from the 1959 Charlton Heston version, with its breakneck chariot race) is a good example of the power, and longevity, of this theme (see Plate 14). It started life as a novel, published in 1880 and subtitled *A Tale of the Christ*, which told the story of Jesus largely through the eyes of a Jew, Judah Ben-Hur, who eventually converts to Christianity. But as the book went through successive adaptations for stage and screen (there were other film versions before the Charlton Heston spectacular) it became increasingly presented as the story of a collision between the worldly power of the Roman state and the upstart Christian subversives, who spread their 'sedition' from the backwater province of Judaea to all the great centres of the empire. It was a provocative scenario, in which audiences could find a parable of power in the modern world—as well as, by 1959, gargantuan epic sets, where the thrills and spills of a civilization both menacingly similar to and quite different from our own could veer alarmingly between exciting chariot races and sadistic executions, spectacular orgies and gladiatorial butchery, humble acts of piety and terrifying persecutions.

So *Classics* can itself be *good to think with*—as well as fun. Again and again, imaginative entertainments and instructive re-creations explore Greek and Roman culture to find orientation for our own world, and to fantasize. Mary Renault's novels *The King Must Die* and *The Bull from the Sea*, for instance, create in mythical prehistoric Crete, long before the era of classical Greece, a weird 'other world', where a society free from 'our' inhibitions (particularly sexual) can be realized. And *Cleopatras* of all sorts, on the page, the stage, or celluloid, from Claudette Colbert to Elizabeth Taylor, have brought the European West a compelling series of visions of the seductions and perversions of the Orient, plus the irresistible formula that ensures that the dominance of Cleopatra over the captivated Mark Antony is always in the end cancelled out by her death; the story always ends with the restoration of proper political order and male supremacy. On the other hand, in the *Asterix* cartoon-strips the tables are turned on the powerful, as the last remnants in the last corner of a free Gaul magically overpower the legions of Caesar, mock the dull wits and flabby physiques of his officers and soldiers, and in the end return to their 'Arcadian' village to feast and sup as (the myth lies) they always will (see Fig. 9).

This jumble of materials in all our media comes to us in no particular order and unsorted. Like all of *Classics* it invites and encourages all kinds of different responses. We may, for example, choose to study the nature of Rome's imperialism, its erosion of national freedoms, and the mechanisms of its military aggression; or we may (at the same time) choose to enjoy the jokes of the cartoon-strip freedom fighters, teaching the dumb conquerors a well-deserved lesson or two. In much the same way, we can poke fun at the image of the priggish Romans, or catch the excitement of Catullus' flip poetry of passion and whim, at the same time as we recognize that no study of ethics, epistemology, or political thought can afford to do without Plato, Aristotle, and Augustine. Even the ancient pagan catch-phrase of 'Christians to the Lions' has found its way into the repertoire of playground jokes ('Christians 0 Lions 250, in a close match'), while still witnessing the suffering of Christian martyrs at the hands of their Roman persecutors.

Classics concerns whole cultures, and the whole range of our responses to those cultures. And so it concerns what is salacious, sordid, or funny, no less than what is informative or improving. Indeed, as we have suggested, the same material from the ancient world may be both funny *and* improving, salacious *and* informative—the difference depending largely on the different questions we choose to ask of it, and on the different ways we frame our responses.

But that *whole range* of responses includes not just our responses to the ancient world itself, but also to the *study* of *Classics*, to the way it is taught, to the educational values it is seen to represent, and to its traditions of scholarship. Here too we find admiration alongside satiric dissent, humour, and even ridicule; here too fiction and the imagination have a part to play—and even (as we shall see) poetry. *Classics*,

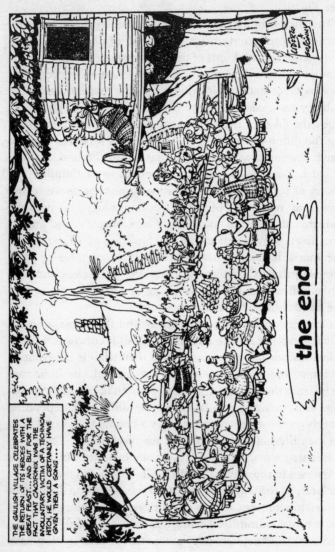

9. Back in Arcadia, with *Asterix the Gladiator*.

and particularly the teaching of the Latin and Greek languages, is deeply embedded in all kinds of modern images of education, schooling, and culture as a whole.

It is well known that old-fashioned schools used to drill the children of the rich in Latin grammar. A hundred years ago in most British public schools not much was taught *except* Latin and Greek. The justification for this was not principally the excitement of the ancient literature that was opened up to a pupil who could read the languages fluently, but the habits of logical rationality that were supposedly inculcated from the careful learning of all the grammatical rules. A minor Victorian industry lay in producing textbooks (some still in use today) to explain the finer points of these rules, to name and describe the grammatical parts: the gerund and gerundive, *amo–amas–amat*, the ablative absolute, the indirect statement, the supine stem of *confiteor*, the conditional sentence in *oratio obliqua*, -μι verbs, the third-person singular pluperfect passive subjunctive of the fourth conjugation (see Fig. 10).

Only a lunatic fringe now believes that the learning of grammatical rules has any positive effect on a pupil's logical thinking. But it is still a matter of debate how the Latin and Greek languages should best (and most enjoyably) be taught. There are now plenty of alternative methods on offer; but they are not our concern here. Our point is rather to emphasize that the teaching of ancient languages has never, even under the Victorian regime, been so monolithic or uncontested as might at first appear. It has always provoked varied responses; and these responses too we should see as part of *Classics*.

Geoffrey Willans and Ronald Searle's comic hero Nigel Molesworth gives us one side of this (see Fig. 11). In the middle of *How to be Topp*, one of the series of Molesworth satires on *skool*, a page of cartoons illustrates 'The Private Life of the Gerund', a Latin grammatical form neatly trans-

And when I asked him the
supine stem of confiteor the fool
didn't know

10. Confessions of a Latin teacher?

formed into an exotic animal, here shown in the hands of
Benjamin Hall Kennedy, the author of the most famous
textbook of Latin grammar ever used in schools. (For one of
Kennedy's handy rhymes to help you learn, see Fig. 12.) The
image shows an endangered species being taken into protection or a freak captured for a circus show—or both. It is, in
any case, a useful reminder that from the moment Latin
grammar was first drilled into the heads of schoolchildren
(willing or unwilling), there was a counter-culture of retaliation in the form of cartoons and graffiti circulating round
the classroom. That imaginative counter-culture has always
been as much a part of the subject as the grammar itself.

But it is not only a matter of schoolboy retaliation. Even
some of those most committed to the study of *Classics* often
paused to wonder about the values and priorities of the

Kennedy discovers the gerund and leads it back into captivity

11. Rote learning of Latin grammar was once nicknamed 'the gerund grind'. Part of the point is that the gerund (a form of a verb functioning as a noun), is rarely found in Latin texts; but it is a star in grammar books such as Kennedy's *Primer*.

> To Nouns that cannot be declined
> The Neuter Gender is assigned:
> Examples fās and nefās give
> And the Verb-Noun Infinitive:
> Est summum nefās fallere:
> *Deceit is gross impiety*.

12. This jingle was *supposed* to help children learn general rules about Latin nouns; but Kennedy does not miss the opportunity to inculcate a moral, too.

narrowest forms of grammatical teaching. The poet Louis MacNeice was a classicist by profession, friend and, for a time, colleague of E. R. Dodds; he learned Latin and Greek at Marlborough College in the 1920s, went on to study Classics at Merton College, Oxford, then taught the subject at

Birmingham and London Universities. In his autobiographical poem 'Autumn Journal', he ironically reflects on how he himself was taught the languages, and on the combination of the prestige of the subject with its stylized artificiality and rote-learning:

> *Which things being so*, as we said when we studied
>   The classics, I ought to be glad
> That I studied the classics at Marlborough and Merton,
>   Not everyone here having had
> The privilege of learning a language
>   That is incontrovertibly dead,
> And of carting a toy-box of hall-marked marmoreal phrases
>   Around in his head.

This is not a criticism of classical teaching made from the outside. It is part of a debate *within Classics* on how the subject should be taught, as well as (now) a representation *of* the subject by one of the most famous poets of the twentieth century. As such, it helps us to see why *Classics* must also include the study *of Classics*.

10 *'Et in Arcadia Ego'*

*I*n the centre of Virgil's 'Arcadian' *Eclogues* is a poem in which two herdsmen exchange songs to mark the death of the archetypal, mythical singer, Daphnis, their inspiration. The second of these songs, forming the second half of the poem, lifts Daphnis to the stars, where he crosses the threshold of Mount Olympus to join the company of the gods, and a new age of peace begins for an eternally thankful countryside. The song promises praise, until time runs down. The first singer mourns the cruel passing of young Daphnis, commemorates his teachings, and laments the devastation of the countryside. His dirge ends, in the middle of Virgil's poem, by organizing a tomb for Daphnis, and an epitaph to be inscribed upon it. This tiny poem will be a song included within the herdsman's song, itself inscribed in the poem-song of Virgil:

> *DAPHNIS EGO IN SILVIS HINC USQUE AD SIDERA NOTUS*
> *FORMOSI PECORIS CUSTOS, FORMOSIOR IPSE.*

> I, DAPHNIS, WELL-KNOWN IN THE WOODLAND FROM HERE
>   RIGHT TO THE STARS,
> HERDSMAN OF A LOVELY FLOCK, AND LOVELIER STILL MYSELF.

In early seventeenth-century Rome, a humanist cardinal, later Pope Clement IX, found inspiration in the proud frag-

ility of this epitaph and emulated the haunting incomplete-
ness of its grammar in coining the proverbial phrase that is
the title of this chapter. ET IN ARCADIA EGO (the sequence of
words runs literally: AND/EVEN IN ARCADIA I) has captured the
imagination of artists and poets throughout western culture
ever since. Its story tells, as we shall see, of death and
paradise. It offers a classical image of our inclusion in, and
exclusion from, the world of the past. At the same time it is
a classical image of the inclusion and exclusion of the
classical world in and from the *Arcadian* world it displaced
and forgot, then remembered, when it was virtually lost. Yes,
we want readers to wonder what this Latin tag is doing at the
head of this final chapter.

In 1786 the classicizing writer and polymath Goethe (J.
Wolfgang von Goethe, then aged 37) left his position in the
government of Weimar for a two-year Grand Tour to Italy,
where he went through an intense experience of awakening,
accompanied by a feverish burst of writing. This experience
and the surge in his life that followed his stay in Italy he
recounted in his *Italian Travels*, entitling one poignant chapter *Auch ich in Arkadien* (a German rendering of the famous
phrase). Now an enthusiastic collector of classical *objets* and
mementos, he poured out streams of sensual *Roman Elegies*
for the young mistress Christiane that he found on his return, working, appropriately enough, in an artificial flower-
factory. Goethe continued to play the part of the responsible
man of affairs, but his heart always lay aeons away from the
round of revolutionary and counter-revolutionary wars and
princes in middle Europe. In the course of his long life he
went on to inspire the Hellenizing strain of Romanticism
that set young men off to rediscover and swoon over the
Greek landscape, its ruins and remains—among them Byron, and Cockerell and his friends. Goethe signals his romantic and nostalgic engagement with the classical world
not least in that chapter title.

A later version of such nostalgia turns up in the tradition of the thoughtless young rake sowing his wild oats, only later to recollect his lost youth in sentimental longing. The cardinal's lapidary phrase carried this idea into the twentieth century, for example, when the young Oxford toffs of Evelyn Waugh's *Brideshead Revisited* monkey around in their rooms with a skull inscribed on its forehead, ET IN ARCADIA EGO, (which is also the title of the novel's 'Book One'). They thought to mock a stuffy cliché, but in the narrator Charles Ryder's retrospect from middle age the uncanny phrase turns out to mock *them*, for the cliché they were living unawares. Put the circle of Lord Marchmain's second son, Sebastian Flyte, into the novel's context in 1945 at the end of the Second World War, and you will appreciate the Arcadian irony when their aesthete friend Anthony B-B-Blanche recites to the young men classic verses of despair taken from T. S. Eliot's 'The Waste Land'. Everything had passed them by (see Fig. 13).

Many of the most famous explorations of ET IN ARCADIA EGO have, however, been in painting. The most famous of them all is the master painter Nicolas Poussin's *Arcadian Shepherds*, commissioned by the very cardinal who had coined the phrase (see Fig. 14). Here a group of young Arcadians gather round a tombstone, intently studying the words, barely decipherable, inscribed upon it—apparently pointing out what they can see to a majestic female figure standing beside them. But for the moment we shall concentrate on a later painting, one that introduced this particular genre to British art: a double portrait of Mrs Bouverie and Mrs Crewe by Sir Joshua Reynolds painted in 1769 (see Plate 15).

Reynolds has one lady point questioningly to the inscription on a tombstone, while the other ponders it in deep contemplation: ET IN ARCADIA EGO strikes again. This was one of Reynolds's first batch of canvases as President of the Royal Academy (an institution that was his brain-child and

13. Another Arcadia: the gilded youth of a bygone age

that had just been formally established in 1768, the idea being to organize the artistic education of British High Society). The story goes that he showed the picture to his friend Dr Johnson (from 1770 the Academy's first Professor of Ancient Literature), who was puzzled, finding the phrase 'nonsensical—I am in Arcadia'. What could *that* mean? The artist retorted that King George III had instantly got the idea the previous day: 'Ay, ay', he had exclaimed, 'death is even in Arcadia.'

This instructive anecdote shows us that the proverbial slogan is more than just grammatically incomplete. Its *meaning* must be supplied, whether by the one who recites it, by those who hear or read it, or by a combination of both. On the one hand, there is the kind of joyous enthusiasm

14. Reynolds's portrait of Mrs Bouverie and Mrs Crewe (see Plate 15) re-works the scheme of *Poussin's Arcadian Shepherds*, in which a group of Arcadian characters surround a tomb. Can they make anything of the famous phrase: ET IN ARCADIA EGO?

which Goethe would proudly proclaim: in his version, he took over the 'I' of the EGO as referring to himself; he imagined a first-person verb; and he produced the sense I TOO HAVE BEEN IN ARCADIA—by which he meant I TOO HAVE BEEN TO PARADISE. This amounts to a romantic nostalgia, placing memories of Arcadian bliss above the dejections of the present. Dr Johnson, on the other hand, plays his given role of the scholar-critic obsessed with words (he did, after all, produce the first systematic dictionary of the English language) and blind to pictorial meaning. He can see none of the clues that led the king (destined to a long dotage of senile dementia) at once to spot that there was someone else to attach to the EGO of the painting's inscription.

The voice, as the king saw, comes from the tomb; so it must be Death speaking: EVEN IN PARADISE AM I. SO THERE IS NO ESCAPE FROM DEATH—EVEN IN ARCADIA. This interpretation has the advantage of suiting the setting of the inscription on the *tomb*. It also correctly construes the Latin (supplying SUM, I AM). But the painting does not simply wish us to take the meaning and run—with one more *memento mori* for our classical collection. For one thing, we should also be remembering the dead Daphnis of Virgil's *Eclogues* when we look at this text, and contemplating *him* as its EGO. If the dead herdsman is saying EVEN IN ARCADIA WAS I, then he must mean: EVEN IN ARCADIA, WHERE I LIVED MY LIFE, I MET MY DEATH AND NOW I AM NO MORE. (To supply FUI, I AM DEAD, is also correct Latin.) Even the loveliest of shepherds, the loveliest of singers, is mortal; and so must we all die.

Every reading of these four, apparently simple, words of Latin is problematic. And *that*, in fact, is what the paintings tell us. For the scenario invented by Poussin, and borrowed by Reynolds to inaugurate a respectful and enquiring classicism in British culture, pours most of its energy into framing the proverb with signals that *writing* is not something we should take for granted. One of Reynolds's ladies needs the other to interpret the marks on the surface of the tomb: her companion may understand all too well, or she may be stuck also—or still be making up her mind. Whichever you choose, the difference between the figures in the picture presses viewers to feel how *the difficulty of reading* intervenes between us and the meaning of the painting.

In order to know what is contained within the painting, its viewer must recognize that the picture *dramatizes* the formula ET IN ARCADIA EGO. In order to know what is contained within the tomb, these painted ladies must read its inscription—and, specifically, they must know some Latin. But they must *also* know the genre of their painting. For they are playing the roles of Poussin's Arcadian shepherds, who point out the letters on *their* tomb, to their own stately female onlooker. In Arcadia we scarcely expect *literate* herdsmen; yet Arcadia is essentially the Virgilian 'elsewhere' known to us—as to Reynolds' ladies—from our reading of the poetic texts of the classical tradition. And among those texts, as we saw at the start of this chapter, is the writing promised for Daphnis' tomb.

The more we find ourselves wondering how writing intersects between our world and Arcadia, the more we shall find that the very writing which distances us from the dead past, also keeps it alive. Think for a moment of the scholars who have between them done most to show the twentieth century the complexities of the painterly genre of ET IN ARCADIA EGO. On the one hand, (Sir) Anthony Blunt, whose painstaking work on the paintings of Poussin provides us with the detail through which we can enter into the artistic imagining of Arcadias in the seventeenth century, and since: perhaps *the* British art-historian of his generation, Surveyor of the Queen's Pictures, and all along, we now know, nursing his secret identity as master-spy for the Soviet Union. On the other hand, Erwin Panofsky, the cultural critic and pre-eminent art-historian of the United States, who was in the 1930s (like Hermann Broch) given asylum there as a refugee from the Nazi persecution of the Jews in Germany. One of Panofsky's classic essays built on Blunt's pre-war research on Poussin to explore the whole story of ET IN ARCADIA EGO, from Virgil onwards.

Blunt received his classical education at school at Marlborough, a contemporary and friend of Louis MacNeice. We have already noticed the scathing sarcasm that MacNeice turned on his training there in the Latin and Greek languages. The same irreverent streak led him to note in his diary after a school visit to the British Museum, that he had been to the Bassae Room and seen the '*Phrig*aleian' marbles. Throughout his career MacNeice's poetry drew widely on classical themes, as well as exploring the art-historical concerns he shared with Blunt into later life. He addresses precisely the issues we are exploring in this chapter in pieces such as the sardonic 'Pindar is Dead', where he sees this most difficult of Greek poets inevitably smothered by the sordid din of modern life: 'There are hikers on the roads | —Pindar is dead— | The petrol pumps are doing a roaring business . . .'; the saccharine 'Poussin', where the painter's 'clouds are like golden tea . . .'; and the 'Eclogue by a five-barred gate', where Death tells two dumbfounded herdsmen, 'There is no way here, shepherds, read the wooden sign, | Your road is a blind road, all this land is mine . . .'

True, MacNeice deprecates his classical education, but when he deplores the contemporary world in which he can find no role for it, his work also insists, with full and knowing irony, on damning that world as barbaric and nasty for, exactly, having no place for the classical heritage. He even puts this in terms which directly revive classical modes for deploring the world. The poet finds modern culture *littered* with classical ruins, fragments, and jumble. He knows, too, that he is programmed to find this; and he understands that the same is true for every educated person in the West who knows that it is only the backdrop of their cultural past that can provide a frame within which they can situate and recognize themselves. Another version of the same lesson is implicit in the sheer range of the knowledge employed in Blunt's and Panofsky's investigations into ET IN ARCADIA EGO.

Panofsky was brought up on *Classics*, too, in a German tradition still more venerable than that of Blunt and MacNeice. He subtly portrays the typical schoolteacher of his day as 'a man of many shortcomings, now pompous, now shy, often neglectful of his appearance, and blissfully ignorant of juvenile psychology'. All he wants to say of the man who taught him Latin is that he was a first-rate specialist on the speeches of Cicero; but Greek he was taught by a 'lovable pedant'. Apologizing for overlooking a misplaced comma in a passage from Plato the pupils were translating, this teacher told his class of 15-year-olds: 'It is my error and yet I wrote an article on this very comma twenty years ago; now we must do the translation over again.' This story stayed alive in Panofsky's mind; indeed he has made it a story *about Panofsky*. It tells us to sift through and find there scrupulous love of learning, as well as pedantic silliness—and then to sort out where *we* stand. And, more generally, the story shows that teachers teach their pupils the way that they themselves learn, whether the pupils choose to imitate, modify, or reject the model. What pupils learn, we learn from Panofsky, is the *process* of learning. Blunt, MacNeice, and Panofsky, in their very different ways, were fully conscious of the complex and vital role that their induction to *Classics* continued to play in their work and their thinking.

The study of *Classics* is never a post-mortem, however 'dead' anyone may call the ancient languages and the cultures which spoke them. So much of Western culture turns on centuries of exploration of the legacy of the classical world that it lies *somewhere* at the roots of pretty well all we can say, see, or think. ET IN ARCADIA EGO is *now*, as you will have realized, a motto for you to complete and situate in relation to yourself. Maybe it is a message of doom, maybe it's a comfort; it might promise you bliss, once you can say the words and mean them; or it may encourage you to keep on thinking, about the life of the past in the present, about the present living in its past. We hope these pages have given some idea of how difficult it is for Western Art, Literature, History, Philosophy, and the rest of our cultural heritage, to speak to our lives without, at the very least, *A Very Short Introduction* to *Classics*.

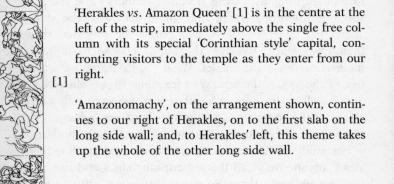

'Herakles *vs.* Amazon Queen' [1] is in the centre at the left of the strip, immediately above the single free column with its special 'Corinthian style' capital, confronting visitors to the temple as they enter from our right.

[1]

'Amazonomachy', on the arrangement shown, continues to our right of Herakles, on to the first slab on the long side wall; and, to Herakles' left, this theme takes up the whole of the other long side wall.

THE FRIEZE FROM THE TEMPLE OF APOLLO AT BASSAE

In this strip we have arranged outline drawings of sculpture which lined the upper walls of the main chamber inside the Temple of Apollo at Bassae. We follow the order presented in the Bassae Room of the British Museum. Our discussion in Chapter 7 explains the significance of this frieze further.

'Lapithocentauromachy' occupies the rest of the long side wall to the right of Herakles, as well as most of the short side on the right of the strip, which ran above the visitor's head on entry, and was visible on exit from the temple,

'Apollo and Artemis' [2] drive into action at our bottom right, as if signalling us to start viewing along the long side from bottom right to left. They also separate the two scenarios: but at the opposite top left corner, the myths simply abut. If Apollo seems 'cornered' in his own shrine, remember that his great statue lurked in the opposite corner of his inner chamber at ⊠, beyond the frieze on the screen of columns.

[2]

The strip is after that in Brian C. Madigan, *The Temple of Apollo Bassitas, Volume II* (Princeton, 1992), though his arrangement of the 23 slabs (devised with Frederick A. Cooper) is very different. Their solution to the 'jigsaw puzzle' was tried out with the frieze at a special British Museum Conference in 1991.

Timelines

c.60–55	Catullus' Love Poetry
	Lucretius' *On the Nature of Things*
44	The dictator Julius Caesar assassinated
43	Legalized murder of Cicero
c.40–35	Gallus' *Elegies*
	Virgil's *Eclogues*
	Varro's *On Farming*

31 BCE-14 CE	**Reign of Augustus**
31 BCE-*c*.500 CE	**Imperial Rome**
31	Octavian's defeat of Antony and Cleopatra
c.31–17 CE	Livy's *History* of Rome
27–23	Augustus' 'restoration' of the Republic (= his Principate)
23	Horace's *Odes*
c.20	Vitruvius' treatise *On Architecture*
19	Death of Virgil, his unfinished *Aeneid* published
c.12	Horace's *Epistles II*
c.1–17 CE	Ovid's *Metamorphoses* and *Fasti*
100–20	Tacitus' *Historical Works*
	Juvenal's *Satires*
122–8	Hadrian's Wall built
c.160	Pausanias' *Guidebook to Greece*

***c*.500–600**	**Collapse of Roman Empire in Western Europe**
***c*.1300–1600**	**Renaissance**
c.1300–15	Dante Alighieri's Italian epic, *Divine Comedy*
1502	Jacopo Sannazaro's romantic poem, *Arcadia*
1592	Sir Philip Sidney's sonnet sequence, *Arcadia*
1599	Shakespeare's *Julius Caesar* first performed

Seventeenth Century

1600–69	Life of Pope Clement IX (Papacy 1667–9)
1638–40	Nicolas Poussin's *Arcadian Shepherds* painted

Eighteenth Century

1748	Pompeii rediscovered
1753	British Museum founded
1765	Bassae rediscovered by Joachim Bocher
1768	Joshua Reynolds sets up Royal Academy

1769	Reynolds's *Mrs Bouverie and Mrs Crewe* painted
1770	Dr Johnson becomes Professor at Royal Academy
1768–88	Goethe's Italian Travels; writes his *Italian Journey*
1783	US Independence recognized
1789	French Revolution
1795	Goethe's *Roman Elegies*
*c.*1750–1820	George Washington, Thomas Jefferson, and Founding Fathers establish USA

Nineteenth Century

*c.*1800–29	Napoleonic Wars and Greek War of Independence from Turkey
	Keats's poetry
	Byron's poetry
1806	Edward Dodwell's visit to Bassae
1811	Sculptures from temple of Aphaia on Aegina excavated and taken to Munich
	'Elgin' marbles taken from Parthenon to British Museum
1811–15	C. R. Cockerell and friends excavate temple at Bassae
	Frieze taken to British Museum (welcomed by Benjamin Haydon)
1829	Edgar Allan Poe's poem *'To Helen'*
1847	B. H. Kennedy's *The Child's Latin Primer* first published
1848	Thomas de Quincey's *Modern Greece*
	Edward Lear visits Bassae
1859	Edward Lear's *The Temple of Apollo at Bassae* installed in Fitzwilliam Museum
1840–80	Karl Marx's political works written and published
*c.*1870–80	Heinrich Schliemann's excavations; discovers sites of Troy and Mycenae
1872–9	Friedrich Nietzsche elaborates philosophy and theory of Tragedy

1880	(General) Lew(is) Wallace's novel, *Ben-Hur. A Tale of the Christ*
1890	J. G. Frazer visits Bassae
1898	J. G. Frazer's *Pausanias*
1896–1909	Lewis Farnell's *Cults of the Greek States*
*c.*1897–1939	Sigmund Freud's psychoanalytic works

Twentieth Century

1910–15	J. G. Frazer's *Golden Bough* published (twelve-volume edition)
1922–43	Mussolini's Fascist regime in Italy
1929	J. G. Frazer's *Fasti*
1933	Erwin Panofsky to USA (refugee from Nazis)
	H. D. Kitto's *In the Mountains of Greece*
1934	Claudette Colbert's *Cleopatra*
	Robert Graves's *I, Claudius* and *Claudius the God*
1936	Erwin Panofsky's essay on *Et in Arcadia Ego*
1938	Anthony Blunt's essay on Poussin's *Et in Arcadia Ego*
*c.*1925–60	Louis MacNeice's poetry
	T. S. Eliot's *The Waste Land*
1945	Hermann Broch's *Death of Virgil*
	Evelyn Waugh's *Brideshead Revisited*
1951	E. R. Dodds's *Greeks and the Irrational*
1954	Geoffrey Willans and Ronald Searle's *How to be Topp*
1956	Mary Renault's *The Last of the Wine*
1958	Willans and Searle's *Down with Skool!*
	Mary Renault's *The King Must Die*
1959	*Ben-Hur* film starring Charlton Heston
1962	Elizabeth Taylor stars in *Cleopatra*
	Mary Renault's *The Bull from the Sea*
1964	R. Goscinny and A. Uderzo's *Asterix the Gladiator*
1972	Simon Raven's *Come Like Shadows*
1980	Umberto Eco's *The Name of the Rose*
1981	Charles Segal's *Tragedy and Civilisation*
1987	Temple of Apollo at Bassae enclosed in a tent

Citations and Further Reading

Chapter 1

Further Reading: BRITISH MUSEUM: Ian Jenkins, *Archaeologists and Aesthetes: In the Sculpture Galleries of the British Museum 1800–1939* (London, 1992); Lucilla Burn, *The British Museum Book of Greek and Roman Art* (London, 1991). HERITAGE: Graeme W. Clarke (ed.), *Rediscovering Hellenism* (Cambridge, 1989); Carol G. Thomas (ed.), *Paths from Ancient Greece* (Leiden, 1988).

Chapter 2

References: Thomas de Quincey, 'Modern Greece', *Collected Works* (2nd ed., Edinburgh, 1863), vol. 13, 288; Byron, 'John Keats, who was kill'd off by one critique': *Don Juan*, Canto XI, stanza LX; Byron, 'But who, of all the plunderers . . .': *Childe Harold's Pilgrimage*, Canto II, stanza XI; Horace and Greek conquest: *Epistles* II.1, verse 156.

Further Reading: REDISCOVERY: Fani-Maria Tsigakou, *The Rediscovery of Greece. Travellers and Painters of the Romantic Era* (London, 1981); Roland and Françoise Etienne, *The Search for Ancient Greece* (London, 1992); Claude Moatti, *The Search for Ancient Rome* (London, 1993); Robert Etienne, *Pompeii. The Day a City Died* (London, 1992). KEATS: Martin Aske, *Keats and Hellenism* (Cambridge, 1985).

Chapter 3

References: H. D. F. Kitto, *In the Mountains of Greece* (London, 1933), 60, 92. Simon Raven, *Come Like Shadows* (London, 1972), 180–3. TOUR GUIDES: *Essential Mainland Greece* (Basingstoke, 1994); *Thomas Cook's Travellers' Mainland Greece, including Athens* (Basingstoke, 1995); *Visitor's Guide. Greece*

(Ashbourne, 1994); *Greece. The Rough Guide* (London, 1995). Virgil, 'uarium et mutabile semper femina', *Aeneid*, Book IV, line 569.

Further Reading: TOURISM: Robert Eisner, *Travelers to an Antique Land. The History and Literature of Travel to Greece* (Michigan, 1991); Helen Angelomatis-Tsougarakis, *The Eve of the Greek Revival. British Travellers' Perceptions of Early Nineteenth-Century Greece* (London, 1990); S. Zinovieff, 'Hunters and Hunted: *Kamaki* and the Ambiguities of Predation in a Greek Town', in Peter Loizos and Evthumios Papataxiarchis (eds.), *Contested Identities: Gender and Kinship in Modern Greece* (Princeton, 1993). THE OTHER: Edith Hall, *Inventing the Barbarian* (Oxford, 1989). MULTICULTURALISM: G. Karl Galinsky, *Classical and Modern Interactions* (Texas, 1993). GENDER: David M. Halperin, John J. Winkler, Froma I. Zeitlin (eds.), *Before Sexuality, The Construction of Erotic Experience in the Ancient Greek World* (Princeton, 1990); A. Richlin (ed.), *Pornography and Representation in Greece and Rome* (Oxford, 1992); Robert Aldrich, *The Seduction of the Mediterranean. Writing, Art and Homosexual Fantasy* (London, 1993); Nancy S. Rabinowitz and Amy Richlin (eds.), *Feminist Theory and the Classics* (London, 1993).

Chapter 4

References: Pausanias' description of Bassae: *Guidebook to Greece*, Book VIII, chapter 41 §§ 7–8—translated in J. G. Frazer, *Pausanias' Description of Greece* (London, 1898), i. 427–8; commentary, iv. 393–405. DESCRIPTIONS OF PLAGUE: Thucydides, *History of the Peloponnesian War*, Book II, chapters 47–54; Lucretius, *On the Nature of Things*, Book VI, verses 1138–1286. GALLUS FRAGMENT: papyrus found at Qasr Ibrîm, 78-3-11/1, see R. D. Anderson, Peter J. Parsons, and Robin G. M. Nisbet, 'Elegiacs by Gallus from Qasr Ibrîm', in *Journal of Roman Studies*, 69 (1979), 125–55. JUVENAL: 'What street isn't awash . . .', *Satire* II, lines 8–13. Robert Graves, *I, Claudius*, and *Claudius the God* (London, 1934). Umberto Eco, *The Name of the Rose* (London, 1980).

Further Reading: PAUSANIAS: Jas Elsner, *Art and the Roman Viewer* (Cambridge, 1995), chapter 4. ANCIENT TEXTS: L. D.

Reynolds and N. G. Wilson, *Scribes and Scholars: A Guide to the Transmission of Greek and Latin Literature* (Oxford, 1991). SCHLIEMANN: William M. Calder and David A. Traill (eds.), *Myth, Scandal, and History: The Heinrich Schliemann Controversy* (Detroit, 1986).

Chapter 5

References: TRANSPORT ESTIMATES: M. I. Finley, *The Ancient Economy* (London, 1973), 126. Varro, 'instrumenti genus uocale', *On Farming*, Book I, chapter 17, § 1. ESTIMATES OF SLAVES: Paul Cartledge, *The Greeks* (Oxford, 1993), 135 ff.; P. A. Brunt, *Italian Manpower* (Oxford, 1971), 124 ff. SLAVERY: Keith Bradley, *Slavery and Society at Rome* (Cambridge, 1994). FIELD SURVEY: Susan E. Alcock, *Graecia Capta* (Cambridge, 1993). ARCHAEOLOGY: Ian Morris (ed.), *Classical Greece. Ancient Histories and Modern Archaeologies* (Cambridge, 1994).

Chapter 6

Reference: Tacitus, Britain shaped as 'scapula': *Life of Agricola*, chapter 10, § 3, ed. R. M. Ogilvie and I. A. Richmond (Oxford, 1967), 168–70. Virgil, Aeneas, and the golden bough, *Aeneid*, Book VI, lines 146–7.

Further Reading: CLASSICAL EDITIONS: E. J. Kenney, *The Classical Text* (Berkeley, 1974). SHAKESPEARE: Charles and Michelle Martindale, *Shakespeare and the Uses of Antiquity* (London, 1994). RENAISSANCE: Isabel Rivers, *Classical and Christian Ideas in English Renaissance Poetry* (London, 1994). J. G. FRAZER: Robert Fraser, *The Making of the Golden Bough: The Origins and Growth of an Argument* (Basingstoke, 1990). FREUD: S. Freud, *Art and Literature* (Harmondsworth, 1985). POLITICS: George E. McCarthy (ed.), *Dialectics and Decadence. Echoes of Antiquity in Marx and Nietzsche* (London, 1994).

Chapter 7

References: REACTIONS TO THE FRIEZE: Edward Dodwell, *A Classical and Topographical Tour through Greece* (London, 1819), 387; M. Robertson, *A History of Greek Art* (Cambridge, 1975);

Benjamin Robert Haydon, quoted by J. G. Frazer, *Pausanias' Description of Greece* (London, 1898), iv. 401.

Further Reading: BASSAE: Charles R. Cockerell, *The Temples of Jupiter Panhellenius at Aegina, and of Apollo Epicurius at Bassae near Phigaleia in Arcadia* (London, 1860). TEMPLES AND RELIGION: Louise Bruit Zaidman and Pauline Schmitt Pantel, *Religion in the Ancient Greek City* (Cambridge, 1992); Pat E. Easterling and John V. Muir, (eds.) *Greek Religion and Society* (Cambridge, 1985); Ken Dowden, *Religion and the Romans* (Bristol, 1992). MYTH: Richard L. Gordon (ed.), *Myth, Religion and Society* (Cambridge, 1981); Richard Buxton, *Imaginary Greece* (Cambridge, 1994); J.-P. Vernant, *Mortals and Immortals* (Princeton, 1991). ART: Robert M. Cook, *Greek Art* (Harmondsworth, 1972); Paul Zanker, *The Power of Images in the Age of Augustus* (Ann Arbor, 1988).

Chapter 8

References: Charles Segal, description of Bassae, *Tragedy and Civilisation. An Interpretation of Sophocles* (Harvard, 1981), 1. E. R. Dodds, *The Greeks and the Irrational* (Berkeley, 1951). Aristotle's analysis of tragedy, *The Poetics*. Thucydides, *History of the Peloponnesian War*, Book II, chapters 63 and 62. Mary Renault, *The Last of the Wine* (London, 1956). Plato's Socrates on the tyrant, *The Republic*, Book VIII, p. 565d. Edgar Allan Poe, 'To Helen' in *Collected Works* (ed. T.O. Mabbott, Cambridge, Mass., 1969), I, 163–71.

Further Reading: THOMAS JEFFERSON AND GEORGE WASHINGTON: see Carl J. Richard, *The Founders and the Classics. Greece, Rome, and the American Enlightenment* (Harvard, 1994), 54 and 71 ff. TRAGEDY: Simon Goldhill, *Reading Greek Tragedy* (Cambridge, 1986). SOCRATES: Barry S. Gower and Michael C. Stokes (eds.), *Socratic Questions. The Philosophy of Socrates and its Significance* (London, 1992). ARISTOTLE: G. E. R. Lloyd, *Aristotle: The Growth and Structure of his Thought* (Cambridge, 1969). HISTORY: Paul Cartledge, *The Greeks* (Oxford, 1993); Fergus Millar and Erich Segal (eds.), *Caesar Augustus. Seven Aspects* (Oxford, 1984). GLADIATORS: Carlin A. Barton, *The Sorrows of the*

Ancient Romans. The Gladiator and the Monster (Princeton, 1993). Fascism: Alec Scobie, *Hitler's State Architecture: The Impact of Classical Antiquity* (Pennsylvania, 1990). America: William L. Vance, *America's Rome* (New Haven, 1989); Eric Havelock, 'Plato and the American Constitution', *Harvard Studies in Classical Philology*, 93 (1990), 1 ff.

Chapter 9

References: Herodotus, how Pan assisted the Athenians, *Histories*, Book VI, chapters 105–6; Lucian, later Greek version of story with details about Marathon, *On a Slip in a Greeting* (Opus 65) § 3. Polybius, *History*, IV, chapters 20–1. Louis MacNeice, 'An Eclogue for Christmas', in *Collected Poems*, ed. E. R. Dodds (London, 1966), 33. Horace, Pan and his Arcadian haunts, *Odes*, Book I, poem 17. Fiona Pitt-Kethley, *The Pan Principle* (London, 1994), 28. Jacopo Sannazaro, *Arcadia and Piscatorial Eclogues*, trans. R. Nash (Detroit, 1966). Sir Philip Sidney, *The Countess of Pembroke's Arcadia*, ed. Maurice Evans (Harmondsworth, 1977). Hermann Broch, *The Death of Virgil* (New York, 1945). Lew Wallace, *Ben-Hur. A Tale of the Christ* (London, 1880). Mary Renault, *The King Must Die* (London, 1958), *The Bull from the Sea* (London, 1962). R. Goscinny and A. Uderzo, *Asterix the Gladiator* (Paris, 1964; trans. Leicester, 1973). Geoffrey Willans and Ronald Searle, *Down with Skool!* (London, 1958) and *How to be Topp* (London, 1954). Louis MacNeice, 'Autumn Journal, XIII', in *Collected Poems*, 125.

Further Reading: Olympic Games: M. I. Finley and H. W. Pleket, *The Olympic Games. The First Thousand Years* (Edinburgh, 1976). Pan: Philippe Borgeaud, *The Cult of Pan in Ancient Greece* (Chicago, 1988). Arcadias: T. G. Rosenmeyer, *The Green Cabinet. Theocritus and the European Pastoral Lyric* (California, 1969). Virgil: Paul Alpers, *The Singer of the Eclogues. A Study of Virgilian Pastoral* (Berkeley, 1979); Viktor Pöschl, *The Art of Virgil. Image and Symbol in the Aeneid* (Michigan, 1970). Late Antiquity: Gillian Clark, *Women in Late Antiquity. Pagan and Christian Lifestyles* (Oxford, 1993). Film and Fiction: D. Mayer, *Playing Out the Empire. Ben-Hur and Other Toga Plays and Films*

(Oxford, 1994); Kenneth MacKinnon, *Greek Tragedy into Film* (London, 1986); Mary Hamer, *Signs of Cleopatra: History, Politics, Representation* (London, 1993). EDUCATION: Christopher Stray, *Culture and Discipline: The Transformation of Classics in England 1830–1960* (Oxford, 1996). MACNEICE: Jon Stallworthy, *Louis MacNeice* (London, 1995).

Chapter 10

References: Virgil, epitaph for Daphnis, *Eclogue V*, verses 43–4. J. Wolfgang von Goethe, *Römische Elegien* (1795), *Italienische Reisen* (1816–17), see Humphry Trevelyan, *Goethe and the Greeks* (Cambridge, 1981). Evelyn Waugh, *Brideshead Revisited* (Harmondsworth, 1945), 43 and 34. T. S. Eliot, *The Waste Land* (London, 1940). Nicolas Poussin, 'The Arcadian Shepherds', illustrated in A. Blunt, *Art and Architecture in France 1500–1700* (Harmondsworth, 1953), pl. 131(B). Reynolds, Johnson, and George III anecdote: C. R. Leslie and Tom Taylor, *Life and Times of Sir Joshua Reynolds* (London, 1865), i. 325; retold by Erwin Panofsky, ' "Et in Arcadia Ego": Poussin and the Elegiac Tradition', in *Meaning in the Visual Arts* (New York, 1955), 295–320. Anthony Blunt, 'Poussin's "Et in Arcadia Ego" ', in *Art Bulletin*, 20 (1938), 96 ff. Louis MacNeice, 'Pindar is Dead', 'Poussin', 'Eclogue by a five-barred gate (Death and Two Shepherds)', in *Collected Poems*, 79, 4, and 37.

Further Reading: NEO-CLASSICISM: Hugh Honour, *Neo-Classicism* (Harmondsworth, 1967). PASTORAL: William Empson, *Some Versions of Pastoral* (London, 1950). CLASSICISTS: E. R. Dodds, *Missing Persons, An Autobiography* (Oxford, 1977); K. J. Dover, *Marginal Comment* (London, 1994).

Index

OXFORD

MORE OXFORD PAPERBACKS

This book is just one of nearly 1000 Oxford Paper-backs currently in print. If you would like details of other Oxford Paperbacks, including titles in the World's Classics, Oxford Reference, Oxford Books, OPUS, Past Masters, Oxford Authors, and Oxford Shakespeare series, please write to:

UK and Europe: Oxford Paperbacks Publicity Manager, Arts and Reference Publicity Department, Oxford University Press, Walton Street, Oxford OX2 6DP.

Customers in UK and Europe will find Oxford Paperbacks available in all good bookshops. But in case of difficulty please send orders to the Cash-with-Order Department, Oxford University Press Distribution Services, Saxon Way West, Corby, Northants NN18 9ES. Tel: 01536 741519; Fax: 01536 746337. Please send a cheque for the total cost of the books, plus £1.75 postage and packing for orders under £20; £2.75 for orders over £20. Customers outside the UK should add 10% of the cost of the books for postage and packing.

USA: Oxford Paperbacks Marketing Manager, Oxford University Press, Inc., 200 Madison Avenue, New York, N.Y. 10016.

Canada: Trade Department, Oxford University Press, 70 Wynford Drive, Don Mills, Ontario M3C 1J9.

Australia: Trade Marketing Manager, Oxford University Press, G.P.O. Box 2784Y, Melbourne 3001, Victoria.

South Africa: Oxford University Press, P.O. Box 1141, Cape Town 8000.

A Very Short Introduction

POLITICS

Kenneth Minogue

Since politics is both complex and controversial it is easy to miss the wood for the trees. In this Very Short Introduction Kenneth Minogue has brought the many dimensions of politics into a single focus: he discusses both the everyday grind of democracy and the attraction of grand ideals such as freedom and justice.

'Kenneth Minogue is a very lively stylist who does not distort difficult ideas.'
Maurice Cranston

'a dazzling but unpretentious display of great scholarship and humane reflection'
Professor Neil O'Sullivan, University of Hull

'Minogue is an admirable choice for showing us the nuts and bolts of the subject.'
Nicholas Lezard, *Guardian*

'This is a fascinating book which sketches, in a very short space, one view of the nature of politics . . . the reader is challenged, provoked and stimulated by Minogue's trenchant views.'
Talking Politics

ARCHAEOLOGY

Paul Bahn

'Archaeology starts, really, at the point when the first recognizable 'artefacts' appear—on current evidence, that was in East Africa about 2.5 million years ago—and stretches right up to the present day. What you threw in the garbage yesterday, no matter how useless, disgusting, or potentially embarrassing, has now become part of the recent archaeological record.'

This Very Short Introduction reflects the enduring popularity of archaeology—a subject which appeals as a pastime, career, and academic discipline, encompasses the whole globe, and surveys 2.5 million years. From deserts to jungles, from deep caves to mountain-tops, from pebble tools to satellite photographs, from excavation to abstract theory, archaeology interacts with nearly every other discipline in its attempts to reconstruct the past.

'very lively indeed and remarkably perceptive . . . a quite brilliant and level-headed look at the curious world of archaeology'
Professor Barry Cunliffe,
University of Oxford

BUDDHISM

Damien Keown

'Karma can be either good or bad. Buddhists speak of good karma as "merit", and much effort is expended in acquiring it. Some picture it as a kind of spiritual capital—like money in a bank account—whereby credit is built up as the deposit on a heavenly rebirth.'

This Very Short Introduction introduces the reader both to the teachings of the Buddha and to the integration of Buddhism into daily life. What are the distinctive features of Buddhism? Who was the Buddha, and what are his teachings? How has Buddhist thought developed over the centuries, and how can contemporary dilemmas be faced from a Buddhist perspective?

'Damien Keown's book is a readable and wonderfully lucid introduction to one of mankind's most beautiful, profound, and compelling systems of wisdom. The rise of the East makes understanding and learning from Buddhism, a living doctrine, more urgent than ever before. Keown's impressive powers of explanation help us to come to terms with a vital contemporary reality.'
Bryan Appleyard

A Very Short Introduction

JUDAISM

Norman Solomon

'Norman Solomon has achieved the near impossible with his enlightened very short introduction to Judaism. Since it is well known that Judaism is almost impossible to summarize, and that there are as many different opinions about Jewish matters as there are Jews, this is a small masterpiece in its success in representing various shades of Jewish opinion, often mutually contradictory. Solomon also manages to keep the reader engaged, never patronizes, assumes little knowledge but a keen mind, and takes us through Jewish life and history with such gusto that one feels enlivened, rather than exhausted, at the end.'
Rabbi Julia Neuberger

'This book will serve a very useful purpose indeed. I'll use it myself to discuss, to teach, agree with, and disagree with, in the Jewish manner!'
Rabbi Lionel Blue

'A magnificent achievement. Dr Solomon's treatment, fresh, very readable, witty and stimulating, will delight everyone interested in religion in the modern world.'
Dr Louis Jacobs, University of London

OXFORD

RETHINKING LIFE AND DEATH
THE COLLAPSE OF OUR TRADITIONAL ETHICS

Peter Singer

A victim of the Hillsborough Disaster in 1989, Anthony Bland lay in hospital in a coma being fed liquid food by a pump, via a tube passing through his nose and into his stomach. On 4 February 1993 Britain's highest court ruled that doctors attending him could lawfully act to end his life.

Our traditional ways of thinking about life and death are collapsing. In a world of respirators and embryos stored for years in liquid nitrogen, we can no longer take the sanctity of human life as the cornerstone of our ethical outlook.

In this controversial book Peter Singer argues that we cannot deal with the crucial issues of death, abortion, euthanasia and the rights of nonhuman animals unless we sweep away the old ethic and build something new in its place.

Singer outlines a new set of commandments, based on compassion and commonsense, for the decisions everyone must make about life and death.

OXFORD PAPERBACK REFERENCE

From *Art and Artists* to *Zoology*, the Oxford Paperback Reference series offers the very best subject reference books at the most affordable prices.

Authoritative, accessible, and up to date, the series features dictionaries in key student areas, as well as a range of fascinating books for a general readership. Included are such well-established titles as Fowler's *Modern English Usage*, Margaret Drabble's *Concise Companion to English Literature*, and the bestselling science and medical dictionaries.

The series has now been relaunched in handsome new covers. Highlights include new editions of some of the most popular titles, as well as brand new paperback reference books on *Politics*, *Philosophy*, and *Twentieth-Century Poetry*.

With new titles being constantly added, and existing titles regularly updated, Oxford Paperback Reference is unrivalled in its breadth of coverage and expansive publishing programme. New dictionaries of *Film*, *Economics*, *Linguistics*, *Architecture*, *Archaeology*, *Astronomy*, and *The Bible* are just a few of those coming in the future.

Oxford
Paperback
Reference

THE OXFORD DICTIONARY OF PHILOSOPHY

Edited by Simon Blackburn

* **2,500 entries covering the entire span of the subject including the most recent terms and concepts**

* **Biographical entries for nearly 500 philosophers**

* **Chronology of philosophical events**

From Aristotle to Zen, this is the most comprehensive, authoritative, and up to date dictionary of philosophy available. Ideal for students or a general readership, it provides lively and accessible coverage of not only the Western philosophical tradition but also important themes from Chinese, Indian, Islamic, and Jewish philosophy. The paperback includes a new Chronology.

'an excellent source book and can be strongly recommended . . . there are generous and informative entries on the great philosophers . . . Overall the entries are written in an informed and judicious manner.'
Times Higher Education Supplement

Oxford
Paperback
Reference

THE CONCISE OXFORD DICTIONARY
OF POLITICS

Edited by Iain McLean

Written by an expert team of political scientists
from Warwick University, this is the most authoritative and up-to-date dictionary of politics available.

* Over 1,500 entries provide truly international
  coverage of major political institutions, thinkers
  and concepts

* From Western to Chinese and Muslim political
  thought

* Covers new and thriving branches of the subject, including international political economy,
  voting theory, and feminism

* Appendix of political leaders

* Clear, no-nonsense definitions of terms such as
  veto and subsidiarity

Oxford
Paperback
Reference

THE CONCISE OXFORD COMPANION
TO ENGLISH LITERATURE

*Edited by Margaret Drabble and
Jenny Stringer*

Derived from the acclaimed *Oxford Companion to English Literature*, the concise maintains the wide coverage of its parent volume. It is an indispensable, compact guide to all aspects of English literature. For this revised edition, existing entries have been fully updated and revised with 60 new entries added on contemporary writers.

* **Over 5,000 entries on the lives and works of authors, poets and playwrights**

* **The most comprehensive and authoritative paperback guide to English literature**

* **New entries include Peter Ackroyd, Martin Amis, Toni Morrison, and Jeanette Winterson**

* **New appendices list major literary prize-winners**

From the reviews of its parent volume:

'It earns its place at the head of the best sellers: every home should have one'
Sunday Times